Copyright Law

Student Study Guide

Copyright Law

Student Study Guide

Robert C. Lind
Professor of Law
Southwestern University School of Law

Carolina Academic Press
Durham, North Carolina

ISBN 0-89089-628-3
LCCN 00-101736

CAROLINA ACADEMIC PRESS
700 Kent Street
Durham, North Carolina 27701
Telephone (919) 489-7486
Fax (919) 493-5668
E-mail: cap@cap-press.com
www.cap-press.com

Printed in the United States of America.

To my copyright law professor, Waldo Moore.

Contents

I. BASES FOR PROTECTION OF WORKS UNDER UNITED STATES COPYRIGHT LAW. 1

A. Constitutional Power of Congress to Provide Copyright Protection. 1

B. Economic Basis for United States Copyright Protection. 1

II. PREREQUISITES FOR FEDERAL STATUTORY COPYRIGHT PROTECTION. 2

A. Statutory Requirements. 2

B. Fixation. 2

C. Originality. 4

D. Expression. 9

III. COPYRIGHTABLE SUBJECT MATTER. 13

A. Literary works. 13

B. Musical works. 25

C. Dramatic works. 25

D. Pantomimes and choreographic works. 25

E. Pictorial, graphic and sculptural works. 26

F. Audiovisual works. 29

G. Sound recordings. 30

H. Architectural works. 31

I. Derivative works. 33

J. Compilations. 35

K. Original works not protected by copyright. 39

IV. OWNERSHIP OF COPYRIGHT. 40

A. Distinction between the ownership of the copyright and the ownership of the material object. 40

B. Works of individual authorship. 41

C. Works made for hire. 41

D. Joint works. 48

E. Joint ownership. 52

F. Divisibility of copyright ownership. 52

G. Transfer of copyright ownership. 53

H. Foreign authors. 59

V. PROTECTION OF EXCLUSIVE RIGHTS. 63

A. Reproduction right. 63

B. Adaptation right. 67

C. Public distribution right. 68

D. Public performance right. 70

E. Public display right. 75

F. Digital public performance right for sound recordings. 75

G. Moral rights. 76

VI. FORMALITIES OF PROTECTION. 80

A. Publication and notice requirement. 80

B. Form of notice. 84

C. Registration and deposit. 85

VII. LENGTH OF PROTECTION. 86

A. Duration of works subject to the 1976 Copyright Act. 86

B. Statutory termination of grants. 90

C. Testamentary and intestate disposition of copyrights. 101

VIII. INFRINGEMENT. 101
A. Procedural considerations. 101
B. Direct infringement. 105
C. Indirect infringement. 111
D. Criminal copyright infringement 117
E. Fair use defense. 117
F. Other affirmative defenses. 137
IX. REMEDIES. 145
A. Nonstatutory monetary damages. 145
B. Statutory damages. 146
C. Injunctive relief. 149
D. Impounding and destruction of infringing articles. 151
E. Costs of suit. 152
F. Attorneys fees. 152
X. ENHANCED PROTECTION FOR DIGITAL MATERIALS. 153
A. Digital Millennium Copyright Act. 153
B. Circumvention of copyright protection systems. 153
C. Integrity of copyright management information. 155
D. Civil remedies. 156
E. Criminal penalties. 157

Appendix A: Table of Cases 159
Appendix B: Table of Statutes 185

Copyright Law

I. BASES FOR PROTECTION OF WORKS UNDER UNITED STATES COPYRIGHT LAW.

A. Constitutional Power of Congress to Provide Copyright Protection.

1. "The Congress shall have Power . . . to Promote the Progress of Science and useful Arts, by securing for limited Times to Authors and Inventors the exclusive Right to their respective Writings and Discoveries." U.S. Const. art. I, § 8.

B. Economic Basis for United States Copyright Protection.

1. "[The limited grant of copyright protection] is intended to motivate the creative activity of authors and inventors by the provision of a special reward, and to allow the public access to the products of their genius after the limited period of exclusive control has expired." Sony Corp. v. Universal City Studios, Inc., 464 U.S. 417, 429 (1984).

2. "The economic philosophy behind the clause empowering Congress to grant patents and copyrights is the conviction that encouragement of individual effort by personal gain is the best way to advance public welfare through the talents of authors and inventors in 'Science and useful Arts.'" Mazer v. Stein, 347 U.S. 201, 219 (1954).

3. This economic basis differs from the European view of copyright protection as an inherent inalienable personal right of the creator of a work.

II. PREREQUISITES FOR FEDERAL STATUTORY COPYRIGHT PROTECTION.

A. Statutory Requirements.

"Copyright protection subsists . . . in original works of authorship fixed in any tangible medium of expression. . . ." 17 U.S.C. § 102(a).

B. Fixation.

1. Federal copyright law protects works of authorship which are "fixed." Federal copyright protection automatically attaches to a work once it is "'fixed' in a tangible medium of expression . . . by or under the authority of the author. . . ." 17 U.S.C. § 101; Community For Creative Non-Violence v. Reid, 490 U.S. 730, 737 (1989) ("As a general rule, the author is the party who actually creates the work, that is, the person who translates an idea into a fixed, tangible expression entitled to copyright protection."). Since January 1, 1978, when the current federal copyright law came into effect, state law can protect only those original works of authorship that are not fixed in any tangible medium of expression. *See e.g.* Cal. Civ. Code § 980(a)(1).

   a. A work may be "fixed" in one of two types of material objects, phonorecords or copies.

      (1) Phonorecords are material objects in which sounds, other than those accompanying an audiovisual work, are fixed and from which the sounds can be perceived, reproduced, or otherwise communicated, either directly or with the aid of a machine or device. 17 U.S.C. § 101. *See* ABKCO Music, Inc. v. Stellar Records, Inc., 96 F.3d 60 (2d Cir. 1996) (karaoke CD-ROM on which sounds and visual representations of lyrics were fixed was a copy, not a phonorecord within the grant of § 115's compulsory mechanical license).

      (2) Copies are material objects, other than phonorecords, in which a work is fixed and from which the work can be perceived, reproduced, or otherwise communi-

cated, either directly or with the aid of a machine. 17 U.S.C. § 101. *See* Midway Manufacturing Co. v. Arctic International, Inc., 547 F. Supp. 999 (N.D. Ill.), *aff'd*, 704 F.2d 1009 (7th Cir. 1982), *cert. denied*, 464 U.S. 823 (1983) (audio-visual work component of video game properly fixed in several ROM chips).

b. A work may be fixed by the author or under the authority of the author. 17 U.S.C. § 101 (definition of "fixed"). Neither the Copyright Act nor its legislative history address whether the authorization of the author must arise prior to fixation or whether the author's subsequent ratification of the fixation is sufficient. *See* Paul S. Bilker, *The Showdown Continues at the Circle C Ranch: Non-Preemption of State Copyright Protection for Unfixed Improvisational Works*, 18 S.W.U. L. Rev. 415, 436-39 (1989).

c. The transmission of a work containing sounds or images is deemed "fixed" if a fixation of the work is made simultaneously with its transmission. 17 U.S.C. § 101 (definition of "fixed"). *See* National Football League v. McBee & Bruno's, Inc., 792 F.2d 726 (8th Cir. 1986) (live broadcast of football game was fixed because it was videotaped at the same time it was transmitted to viewers).

d. Once a work is fixed, its subsequent destruction does not vitiate its copyright. Peter Pan Fabrics, Inc. v. Rosstex Fabrics, Inc., 733 F. Supp. 174, 177 (S.D.N.Y. 1990).

e. Placing expression into computer RAM memory may be sufficiently permanent for it to be deemed fixed. *See* MAI Systems Corp. v. Peak Computer, Inc., 991 F.2d 511 (9th Cir. 1993); Advanced Computer Services of Michigan v. MAI Systems, Corp., 845 F. Supp. 356 (E.D. Va. 1994); Ira Brandriss, *Writing in Frost on a Window Pane: E-Mail and Chatting on Ram and Copyright Fixation*, 43 Journal of the Copyright Society of the USA 237 (1996).

f. Performers may sue one who fixes, transmits or distributes the sounds or images of a live musical performance, without the consent of the performer. This is regardless of whether the musical performance was ever fixed by the performer. 17 U.S.C. § 1101.

(1) The federal anti-bootlegging statute criminalizes the unauthorized fixation of and trafficking in sound recordings and music videos of live musical performances. 18 U.S.C. § 2319A. *See* United States v. Moghadam, 175 F.3d 1269 (11th Cir. 1999) (noting that the statute may not meet the fixation and "limited times" requirements of the Copyright Clause, court held the statute valid under the Commerce Clause).

2. Investing a Work with Federal Copyright Protection Under the 1909 Act.

   a. Under the prior 1909 Copyright Act, a work was invested with federal copyright protection when it was published with proper copyright notice, or when it was registered with the United States Copyright Office. Prior to publication, the work was protected by state common law copyright.

   b. Initial publication of a work in a foreign country with a notice of United States copyright invested the work with United States copyright protection for 28 years, with the possibility of an additional 28 years of protection upon renewal of the copyright. *See* Twin Books Corp. v. Walt Disney Co., 83 F.3d 1162, 1168 (9th Cir. 1996).

C. Originality.

1. The constitutional grant of power to Congress to create a system of copyright protection is limited to the protection of "authors". Implicit in the word "authors" is the requirement that the expression be that of the author and not a copy of another's expression. This is the basis for the originality requirement which is codified in 17 U.S.C. § 102(a) ("Copyright protection subsists... in original works of authorship fixed in any tangible medium of expression....").

2. The "author" need not be a natural being. Under the work for hire doctrine a corporation may be deemed the author of a work. *See* 17 U.S.C. § 201(b); Scherr v. Universal Match Corp., 417 F.2d 497, 502 (2d Cir. 1969). The work, however, must have been created by a human. Urantia Foundation v. Maaherra, 114 F.3d 955 (9th Cir. 1997).

3. Dual Test of Originality.

    a. "Original, as the term is used in copyright, means only that the work was independently created by the author (as opposed to copied from other works), and that it possesses at least some minimal degree of creativity." Feist Publications, Inc. v. Rural Telephone Service Company, Inc., 499 U.S. 340, 345 (1991).

    b. Independent Creation.

        (1) An author must be the creator of the elements of the work at issue. One who copies may not claim authorship. "Originality" means "only that the work owes its origin to the author—*i.e.*, that the work is independently created rather than copied from other works." Reader's Digest Ass'n v. Conservative Digest, Inc., 821 F.2d 800, 806 (D.C. Cir. 1987). *See also* Alfred Bell & Co. v. Catalda Fine Arts, Inc., 191 F.2d 99 (2d Cir. 1951) (copyrightability is determined by the standard of originality, rather than the patent standard of novelty).

        (2) Copyright law acknowledges the possibility of independent creation; the notion that the same work could be independently created by two separate authors. *See* Grubb v. KMS Patriots, L.P., 88 F.3d 1, 3 (1st Cir. 1996); Alfred Bell & Co. v. Catalda Fine Arts, Inc., 191 F.2d 99, 103 (2d Cir. 1951). "[I]f by some magic a man who had never known it were to compose anew Keat's Ode on a Grecian Urn, he would be an 'author,' and, if he copyrighted it, others might not copy that poem, though they might of course copy Keat's." Sheldon v. Metro-Goldwyn Pictures Corp., 81 F.2d 49, 54 (2d Cir. 1936). *But*

see Acuff-Rose Music, Inc. v. Josten's, Inc., 155 F.3d 140, 144 (2d Cir. 1998) (given the widespread usage of the phrase "You've got to stand for something," court held it exceedingly unlikely that composer had independently created the phrase).

c. Creativity.

(1) A work to be copyrightable need only contain a modicum of creativity. Feist Publications, Inc. v. Rural Telephone Service Company, Inc., 499 U.S. 340, 345 (1991) ("To be sure, the requisite level of creativity is extremely low; even a slight amount will suffice. The vast majority of works make the grade quite easily, as they possess some creative spark, 'no matter how crude, humble or obvious' it might be."). Expressions which are part of shared public expressions or are deemed too trivial or insignificant will not be granted copyright protection. *See* John Muller & Co. v. New York Arrows Soccer Team, 802 F.2d 989 (8th Cir. 1986) (soccer team logo consisting of four angled lines which form an arrow and the word "arrows" in cursive script below the arrow held to lack the level of creativity needed for copyrightability); Bailie v. Fisher, 258 F.2d 425 (D.C. Cir. 1958) (cardboard star deemed not worthy of copyright protection); Alberto-Culver Co. v. Andrea Dumon, Inc., 466 F.2d 705 (7th Cir. 1972) (fragmentary words and phrases not copyrightable); Atari Games Corp. v. Oman, 888 F.2d 878 (D.C. Cir. 1989) (common geometric shapes are not copyrightable, but the arrangement of common forms may be); 37 C.F.R. § 202.1 (1991) ("familiar symbols or designs" and "mere variations of typographical ornamentation, lettering or coloring" are not subject to copyright protection). However, there is no quality test of copyrightability.

(2) The traditional *de minimis* standard of creativity is that which was enunciated by the Second Circuit: "All that is needed to satisfy both the Constitution

and the statute is that the 'author' contributed something more than a 'merely trivial' variation, something recognizably 'his own.'" Alfred Bell & Co. v. Catalda Fine Arts, Inc., 191 F.2d 99, 102-03 (2d Cir. 1951). *See* Entertainment Research Group, Inc. v. Genesis Creative Group, Inc., 122 F.3d 1211, 1220 (9th Cir. 1997); Maljack Productions, Inc. v. UAV Corp., 964 F. Supp. 1416 (C.D. Cal. 1997), *aff'd*, 160 F.3d 1223 (9th Cir. 1998) ("pan and scan" version of public domain film, *McClintock!*, with enhanced soundtrack held to be sufficiently original for copyright protection). *But see* Gracen v. Bradford Exchange, 698 F.2d 300 (7th Cir. 1983) (A derivative work requires a greater degree of originality than does the underlying work to be protected by copyright; there must be a substantial variation between the derivative work and the underlying work). *See generally* Olson, *Copyright Originality*, 48 Mo. L. Rev. 29 (1983).

(3) No matter how artistically lacking a work may be, it is protectible by copyright. Bleistein v. Donaldson Lithographing Co., 188 U.S. 239, 250 (1903) (aesthetic quality not relevant to copyright protection); Campbell v. Acuff-Rose Music, Inc., 510 U.S. 569 (1994).

4. There are three views regarding the protectible originality of photographs.

   a. In Burrow-Giles Lithographic Co. v. Sarony, 111 U.S. 53 (1884), the Supreme Court found a photograph of Oscar Wilde protectible by focusing on the elements of originality present in front of the lens: posing of the subject, selection and arrangement of costume, draperies and accessories, use of light and shade, evoking the desired expression from the subject.

   b. In Time, Inc. v. Bernard Geis Associates, 293 F. Supp. 130 (S.D.N.Y. 1968), the court found the Zapruder film protectible by analyzing the elements of originality present behind the lens: selection of camera, film and lens, selection of the image to be photographed, the timing of the taking of the photograph, the positioning of the camera and the photographer. *See* Los Angeles News Service v. Tullo, 973 F.2d 791, 794 (9th Cir. 1992) (originality of videotape taken from a helicopter was found in "the choices of the heights and directions from which to tape"). *But see* Bridgeman Art Library, Ltd. v. Corel Corp., 36 F. Supp. 191, 196-97 (S.D.N.Y. 1999) (color transparencies of public domain paintings deemed "slavish copies" that lacked sufficient originality for copyright protection).

c. In Jeweler's Circular Publishing Co. v. Keystone Publishing Co., 274 F. 932, 934 (S.D.N.Y. 1921), *aff'd*, 281 F. 83 (2d Cir.), *cert. denied*, 259 U.S. 581 (1922), Judge Learned Hand opined that every photograph contains original elements of the photographer. "[N]o photograph, however simple, can be unaffected by the personal influence of the author, and no two will be absolutely alike."

5. Originality in Musical Compositions.

   a. Short musical phrases may be protectible by copyright. *See* Santrayll v. Burrell, 39 U.S.P.Q.2d 1052 (S.D.N.Y. 1996) (repetition of the non-protectible word "uh-oh" in a distinctive rhythm comprises a sufficiently original composition to render it protectible by copyright). *But see* Jarvis v. A & M Records, 827 F. Supp. 282, 291 (D.N.J. 1993) (easily arrived at phrases and chord progressions are usually noncopyrightable).

   b. Harmony can be the subject of copyright. Tempo Music, inc. v. Famous Music Corp., 838 F. Supp. 162 (S.D.N.Y. 1994) (choice of particular harmonic relationship can be considered a creative choice protected by copyright as a derivative work).

6. Mechanical transformations such as derivative works resulting from a simple molding process or obvious translations of a limited nature are not protected by copyright.

See, e.g., L. Batlin & Son, Inc. v. Snyder, 536 F.2d 486 (2d Cir. 1976) (copyright in plastic replica of cast-iron "Uncle Sam" bank held invalid); Entertainment Research Group, Inc. v. Genesis Creative Group, Inc., 122 F.3d 1211, 1222-23 (9th Cir. 1997) (differences in form, texture and proportionality between three-dimensional inflatable costumes and the two-dimensional cartoon characters on which they were based stemmed from unprotectible functional considerations); Bridgeman Art Library, Ltd. v. Corel Corp., 36 F. Supp. 191, 196-97 (S.D.N.Y. 1999) (color transparencies of public domain paintings deemed "slavish copies" that lacked sufficient originality for copyright protection); Tempo Music, Inc. v. Famous Music Corp., 838 F. Supp. 162 (S.D.N.Y. 1994) (harmony that is a mechanical by-product of melody is not protected by copyright).

D. Expression.

1. Copyright law protects the expression of ideas, not the ideas themselves. Ideas cannot be protected by copyright. Copyright law does not preclude others from using the ideas revealed by the author's work. Ideas contained in a work are given to the public immediately upon fixation. *See* Baker v. Selden, 101 U.S. 99 (1879); Curtin v. Star Editorial Inc., 2 F. Supp. 2d 670, 674 (E.D. Pa. 1998) (plaintiff could not claim copyright protection for his "idea" to display photographs of Elvis Presley with celebrities). *But see* American Dental Ass'n v. Delta Dental Plans Ass'n, 126 F.3d 977, 979 (7th Cir. 1997) (taxonomy of dental procedures held to be protected expression: "Classification is a creative endeavor.").

2. This rule, regarding the idea/expression dichotomy, is codified by the 1976 Copyright Act: "In no case does copyright protection for an original work of authorship extend to any idea, procedure, system, method of operation, concept, principle, or discovery, regardless of the form in which it is described, explained, illustrated, or embodied in such work." 17 U.S.C. § 102(b).

   a. Individual recipes comprising lists of required ingredients and directions for combining them to achieve final products, without expressive elaboration, constitute a "procedure" and are not entitled to copyright protection. Publications Int'l, Ltd. v. Meredith Corp., 88 F.3d 473, 480-81 (7th Cir. 1996).

b. The menu command hierarchy of a computer spreadsheet program was a "method of operation" that was held not copyrightable under § 102(b). Lotus Development Corp. v. Borland International, Inc., 49 F.3d 807 (1st Cir. 1995), *aff'd by an equally divided Court*, 516 U.S. 233 (1996).

c. Taxonomies have been held not to constitute a "system." *See* American Dental Ass'n v. Delta Dental Plans Ass'n, 126 F.3d 977, 980-81 (7th Cir. 1997).

3. Merger Doctrine.

   a. Where the expression of an idea is inseparable from the idea itself, the expression will not be protected by copyright. Kern River Gas Transmission Co. v. Coastal Corp., 899 F.2d 1458 (5th Cir.), *cert. denied*, 498 U.S. 952 (1990).

   b. Where the subject matter of a work can be expressed only in a limited number of forms of expression, the expression is copyrightable, though it is protected only against verbatim or near verbatim copying. Herbert Rosenthal Jewelry Corp. v. Kalpakian, 446 F.2d 738 (9th Cir. 1971) (jeweled bee deemed limited expression); *but see* Morrissey v. Procter & Gamble Co., 379 F.2d 675 (1st Cir. 1967) (copyright will not protect any of the limited number of expressions). Under the so-called "merger" doctrine, expression will not be protected in those instances where there is only one or so few ways of expressing an idea that protection of the expression would effectively accord protection to the idea itself. Kregos v. The Associated Press, 937 F.2d 700, 705 (2d Cir. 1991).

4. Where both the plaintiff's and the defendant's works reflect a subject found in nature, plaintiff must show, in a copyright infringement action, that the defendant's work

is a near verbatim copy of the plaintiff's work. Streeter v. Rolfe, 491 F. Supp. 416 (W.D. La. 1980) (turkey decoys); Franklin Mint Corp. v. National Wildlife Art Exchange, Inc., 575 F.2d 62 (3d Cir.), *cert. denied*, 439 U.S. 880 (1978) (paintings of cardinals).

5. Blank forms.

   a. Pursuant to the "blank form doctrine," forms that convey no information and serve only to provide blank space for recording information may not be protected by copyright. Baker v. Selden, 101 U.S. 99, 107 (1879); *see* Brown Instrument Co. v. Warner, 161 F.2d 910 (D.C. Cir. 1947) (chart acting as a cooperating part of temperature monitoring machine held not copyrightable). This doctrine is reflected in the regulations of the Copyright Office which preclude the registration of "[b]lank forms, such as time cards, graph paper, account books, diaries, bank checks, scorecards, address books, report forms, order forms and the like, which are designed for recording information and do not in themselves convey information." 37 C.F.R. § 202.1(c) (1992). A work containing a blank form may be copyrightable due to the selection and arrangement of the categories of information to be recorded on the forms or the textual matter accompanying the form. *See* Kregos v. The Associated Press, 937 F.2d 700 (2d Cir. 1991); Bibbero Systems, Inc. v. Colwell Systems, Inc., 893 F.2d 1104 (9th Cir. 1990); Harcourt, Brace & World, Inc. v. Graphic Controls Corp., 329 F. Supp. 517 (S.D.N.Y. 1971).

6. Words and short phrases such as names, titles, and slogans, or the mere listing of ingredients or contents are not protected by copyright. 37 C.F.R. § 202.1 (1998); Shaw v. Lindheim, 919 F.2d 1353, 1362 (9th Cir. 1990) (title of "The Equalizer" television series not protected by copyright); Trenton v. Infinity Broadcasting Corp., 865 F. Supp. 1416, 1426 (C.D. Cal. 1994) (title of "Loveline" radio program not protected by copyright); Perma Greetings, Inc. v. Russ Berrie & Co., Inc., 598 F. Supp. 445, 448 (E.D. Mo. 1984)

("Cliched language, phrases and expressions conveying an idea that is typically expressed in a limited number of stereotypic fashions, are not subject to copyright protection."). *But see* Universal City Studios, Inc. v. Kamar Industries, Inc., 217 U.S.P.Q. 1162 (S.D. Tex. 1982) ("I Love You, E.T." and "E.T. Phone Home" protected by copyright).

7. Submission or disclosure of ideas is not protected by copyright, but may be protected under various state law theories.

   a. Express contract.

      (1) Submission of an idea may be pursuant to an express contract. The disclosure of the idea constitutes sufficient consideration. Liability in a breach of contract case can arise even if a nonsubstantial element of the author's work is copied. *See* Buchwald v. Paramount Pictures Corp., 13 U.S.P.Q.2d 1497 (Cal. Sup. Ct. 1990).

   b. Implied-in-fact contract.

      (1) Under California law, an idea is not property, but a person who conveys a valuable idea to a producer who commercially solicits it or who voluntarily accepts it knowing that it is tendered for a price should be entitled to recover. The law, however, will not imply a promise to pay for an idea from the mere facts that the idea has been conveyed, is valuable, and has been used for profit. The offeree must have had the opportunity to reject the proffered conveyance of the idea before it is conveyed. "The idea man who blurts out his idea without having first made his bargain has no one but himself to blame for the loss of his bargaining power." Desny v. Wilder, 46 Cal. 2d 715, 299 P.2d 257 (1956).

      (2) New York law makes it more difficult to protect the disclosure of an idea. New York analyzes idea disclosure as a form of property. To be protectible the idea must be "novel." *See* Murray v. National Broadcasting Company, Inc., 844 F.2d 988 (2d Cir. 1988) (novelty cannot be found to exist where an

idea consists of nothing more than a variation on a basic theme).

c. Quasi contract—Unjust enrichment.

(1) Even though parties may not have exhibited a mutual manifestation of assent, thereby making an express or implied-in-fact contract unavailable, the law may require a reasonable payment for the use of a disclosed idea as an equitable matter. "Quasi contractual recovery is based upon benefit accepted or derived from which the law implies an obligation to pay." Weitzenkorn v. Lesser, 40 Cal. 2d 778, 794, 256 P.2d 947, 959 (1953).

d. Breach of a confidential relationship.

(1) An action for breach of a confidential relationship will arise when an idea, whether or not protectible, is offered to another in confidence, and is voluntarily received by the offeree in confidence with the understanding that it is not to be disclosed to third persons, and is not to be used by the offeree for purposes unauthorized by the offeror. A confidential relationship will not be created from the mere submission of an idea to another. There must exist evidence of the communication of the confidentiality of the submission or evidence from which a confidential relationship can be inferred. Faris v. Enberg, 97 Cal. App. 3d 309, 158 Cal. Rptr. 704 (1979).

III. COPYRIGHTABLE SUBJECT MATTER.

A. Literary works.

1. Letters, lectures, speeches, manuals, catalogues and corporate documents as well as other traditional prose material such as novels, articles and scripts are protected by copyright. *See e.g.*, Salinger v. Random House, Inc., 811 F.2d 90, 94-95 (2d Cir. 1987) (author of the letter owns the copyright in its contents, while the recipient of the letter retains ownership of the physical document); Grund-

berg v. Upjohn Company, 137 F.R.D. 372, 19 U.S.P.Q.2d 1590 (D. Utah 1991) (litigation documents); Jackson v. MPI Home Video, 694 F. Supp. 483 (N.D. Ill. 1988) (televised speech); City Consumer Services, Inc. v. Horne, 100 F.R.D. 740 (D. Utah 1983) (compilation of business records); Khandji v. Keystone Resorts Management, Inc., 140 F.R.D. 697, 23 U.S.P.Q.2d 1156 (D. Colo. 1992) (settlement brochure); Rexnord, Inc. v. Modern Handling Systems, Inc., 379 F. Supp. 1190 (D. Del. 1974) (manufacturer's catalogue).

2. Mere themes and bare plots are not protected by copyright. Shipman v. RKO Pictures, 100 F.2d 533, 538 (2d Cir. 1938); *see* Sheldon v. Metro-Goldwyn Pictures Corp., 81 F.2d 49, 53 (2d Cir.), *cert. denied*, 298 U.S. 669 (1936); Midas Productions, Inc. v. Baer, 437 F. Supp. 1388, 1390 (C.D. Cal. 1977).

3. Copyright protects not only the words, sentences and paragraphs of a literary work, but also the dialogue, incidents, dramatic devices, sequences of events, and the development of the interplay of characters. Nichols v. Universal Pictures Corp., 45 F.2d 119 (2d Cir. 1930), *cert. denied*, 282 U.S. 902 (1931). In the Ninth Circuit a literary work is deemed to consist of eight concrete elements: plot, themes, dialogue, mood, setting, pace, sequence of events and characters. Shaw v. Lindheim, 908 F.2d 531 (9th Cir. 1990).

   a. Traditionally, the copyright protection of a nonfiction literary work has been limited to its literal elements: words, sentences and paragraphs. *See, e.g.*, Miller v. Universal City Studios, Inc., 650 F.2d 1365 (5th Cir. 1981). *But see* Feist Publications, Inc. v. Rural Telephone Service Co., Inc., 499 U.S. 340 (1991) (sufficiently original selection, coordination and arrangement of facts may be protected by copyright).

4. Scenes a faire.

   a. Incidents, characters or settings which at one time may have been protectible expression, but are now as a practical matter indispensable, or at least standard, in the treatment of a given topic, are no longer protected by copyright. Nelson v. Grisham, 942 F. Supp. 649, 653 (D.D.C. 1996) (presence in the novel, *The Chamber*, of media, politicians and jail house personnel, as well as the frenzy with which last minute appeals are made, "are all stock events and scenes that are expected in any book about the representation of a death row inmate"); Alexander v. Haley, 460 F. Supp. 40, 45 (S.D.N.Y. 1978).

b. Sequences of events that "necessarily result from the choice of a setting or situation" do not enjoy copyright protection. *See* Williams v. Crichton, 84 F.3d 581, 589 (2d Cir. 1996) (setting of a dinosaur zoo or adventure park, with electrified fences, automated tours, dinosaur nurseries, uniformed workers, and placing dinosaurs on a prehistoric island far from the mainland "are classic scenes a faire that flow from the uncopyrightable concept of a dinosaur zoo."); Midas Productions, Inc. v. Baer, 437 F. Supp. 1388 (C.D. Cal. 1977) (non-infringing elements taken by defendant common to the genre of films that depict "young people of the '60s on the move").

5. Conversations.

a. The law is unclear as to when, if ever, a conversation may be protected by copyright. Note that a lecture, which is generally composed prior to its delivery, is not considered to be a conversation and is fully protectible by copyright as a literary work. *See* Jackson v. MPI Home Video, 694 F. Supp. 483, 490 (N.D. Ill. 1988) (Jesse Jackson's speech at the 1988 Democratic Party Convention found protectible as a literary work).

b. The classic "conversation" case is Estate of Hemingway v. Random House, Inc., 23 N.Y.2d 341, 296 N.Y.S.2d 771, 244 N.E.2d 250 (1969). In that case the New York Court of Appeal stated that while there is a presumption that conversations are not copyrightable subject matter, there may be limited and special circumstances where that presumption may be overcome. Under this approach, the speaker may successfully claim copyright protection for her statements under the following conditions: First, the speaker must indicate that she intended to mark off the utterance from the ordinary stream of speech. Second, the speaker must indicate that she meant to adopt the utterance as a unique statement. Third, the speaker must indicate that she wished to exercise the control over the statement's publication.

c. Other courts have taken a very narrow view of copyright protection of conversations. *See* Falwell v. Penthouse International, Ltd., 521 F. Supp. 1204, 1207-08 (W.D. Va. 1981): "Plaintiff's claim of copyright presupposes that every utterance he makes is a valuable property right. If this were true, the courts would be inundated with claims from celebrities and public figures all of whom may argue that their expressions should also be afforded the extraordinary protection of copyright. Such a result was never contemplated by the development of the law regarding common law copyright, and such a result would run counter to the firmly established constitutional guarantees of freedom of speech and of the press." *See also* Marvin Worth Productions v. Superior Films Corp., 319 F. Supp. 1269 (S.D.N.Y. 1970).

6. Facts are not protected by copyright.

   a. Copyright protection extends only to an author's expression of facts and not to the facts themselves. As a policy matter, historical and scientific facts are viewed as building blocks necessary for subsequent authors. Furthermore, a fact does not originate with the author of a book describing the fact. Since facts do not owe their origin to any individual, they are part of the public domain available to every person. Feist Publications, Inc. v. Rural Telephone Service Company, Inc., 499 U.S. 340, 347 (1991) ("[F]acts do not owe their origin to an act of authorship. The distinction is one between creation and discovery: the first person to find and report a particular fact has not created the fact; he or she has merely discovered its existence."); Miller v. Universal City Studios, 650 F.2d 1365 (5th Cir. 1981). Initial scientific discoveries may be protected by patent or trade secret law.

(1) The taking of facts from a protected work does not constitute copyright infringement. *See* Nihon Keizai Shimbun, Inc. v. Comline Business Data, Inc., 166 F.3d 65, 70 (2d Cir. 1999).

b. Interpretation of historical fact is not protected by copyright. Hoehling v. Universal City Studios, Inc., 618 F.2d 972 (2d Cir.), *cert. denied*, 449 U.S. 841 (1980); Chase-Riboud v. Dreamworks, Inc., 987 F. Supp. 1222, 1226 (C.D. Cal. 1997) (scope of copyright in historical accounts is narrow). *But see* Wainwright Securities Inc. v. Wall Street Transcript Corp., 558 F.2d 91 (2d Cir. 1977); Salinger v. Random House, Inc., 818 F.2d 252, 254 (2d Cir. 1987).

c. Historical or scientific research is not protected by copyright. Rosemont Enterprises, Inc. v. Random House, Inc., 366 F.2d 303 (2d Cir. 1966), *cert. denied*, 385 U.S. 1009 (1967). Copyright law will not protect the investment of time, money and energy which research requires. *See* Feist Publications, Inc. v. Rural Telephone Service Company, Inc., 499 U.S. 340, 352-356 (1991).

d. Purported fact, which is actually fictional, will be treated as though it were an actual fact and will receive no copyright protection. Davies v. Bowes, 209 F. 53 (S.D.N.Y. 1913).

e. While the original selection and arrangement of facts in a compilation are protectible, the selection and arrangement of facts in prose have traditionally not been protected. *See* Miller v. Universal City Studios, 650 F.2d 1365 (5th Cir. 1981). The Supreme court's decision in Feist may bring about a change to this traditional rule. *See* Feist Publications, Inc. v. Rural Telephone Service Company, Inc., 499 U.S. 340 (1991).

7. Characters.

   a. There is agreement among the circuit courts of appeal that a graphic character, the physical characteristics of which are seen by the viewer, is more easily copyrightable than is a literary character. The graphic character must be sufficiently fleshed out to constitute more than an idea; more than a stock character. Walt Disney Productions v. Air Pirates, 581 F.2d 751 (9th Cir. 1978); Warner Bros., Inc. v. American Broadcasting Companies., 720 F.2d 231 (2d Cir. 1983) (Greatest American Hero did not infringe on Superman).

   b. Stock or stereotyped characters are not protected by copyright. Reyher v. Children's Television Workshop, 533 F.2d 87 (2d Cir.), *cert. denied*, 429 U.S. 980 (1976); Midas Productions, Inc. v. Baer, 437 F. Supp. 1388, 1390 (C.D. Cal. 1977).

   c. In the majority of jurisdictions literary characters which are sufficiently "fleshed out," with physical traits, personality traits and back story, may be protected by copyright. *See e.g.*, Nichols v. Universal Pictures Corp., 45 F.2d 119 (2d Cir. 1930), *cert. denied*, 282 U.S. 902 (1931); Filmvideo Releasing Corp. v. Hastings, 509 F. Supp. 60 (S.D.N.Y. 1981), *aff'd*, 668 F.2d 91 (2d Cir. 1981); Silverman v. CBS, Inc., 870 F.2d 40 (2d Cir. 1989).

      (1) A character may be protected as a compilation of character traits that individually would not be protected by copyright law. *See* Lone Wolf McQuade Associates v. CBS, Inc., 961 F. Supp. 587 (S.D.N.Y. 1997).

      (2) The Ninth Circuit has distinguished literary characters from graphic characters. Under this approach, graphic characters found in cartoons, comics, motion pictures, television or three dimensional works, are analyzed under the "fleshing out" test. Literary

characters, however, are deemed not protectible under copyright law unless "the character really constitutes the story being told" and is not merely a "chess man in the game of telling the story." Warner Bros. Pictures, Inc. v. Columbia Broadcasting System, Inc., 216 F.2d 945, 950 (9th Cir. 1954). This unique test for literary character protection has been widely criticized and appears to be no longer followed in the Ninth Circuit. *See* Shaw v. Lindheim, 908 F.2d 531 (9th Cir. 1990). *But see* Metro-Goldwyn-Mayer, Inc. v. American Honda Motor Co., Inc., 900 F. Supp. 1287, 1296 (C.D. Cal. 1995) (James Bond character protected under the "story being told" test because "audiences do not watch Tarzan, Superman, Sherlock Holmes, or James Bond for the story, they watch these films to see their heroes at work. A James Bond film without James Bond is not a James Bond film.").

d. A character is only protectible as a part of a literary, musical, dramatic, pictorial or audiovisual work. The Copyright Office will not register a character which is independent of any other work.

e. Copyright protection is extended to the component part of a character which significantly aids in identifying the character. New Line Cinema Corp. v. Eastern Unlimited, Inc., 17 U.S.P.Q.2d 1631 (E.D.N.Y. 1989) (glove with razor fingers significantly aided in identifying Freddy Krueger character).

8. Computer programs.

a. The literal elements of computer operating programs and application programs are copyrightable subject matter. Apple Computer, Inc. v. Franklin Computer Corp., 714 F.2d 1240 (3d Cir. 1983), *cert. dismissed*, 464 U.S. 1033 (1984).

b. The scope of the copyright protection given to computer programs continues to be a dynamic area of copyright law. All courts agree that the literal elements of a computer program, the literal text of the program's instructions written in a particular programming language, are protectible by copyright. *See e.g.*, Johnson Controls, Inc. v. Phoenix Control Systems, Inc., 886 F.2d 1173, 1175 (9th Cir. 1989); Apple Computer, Inc. v. Franklin Computer Corp., 714 F.2d 1240 (3d Cir. 1983), *cert. dismissed*, 464 U.S. 1033 (1984).

c. The scope of protection to be given to the non-literal elements of a computer program continues to be in dispute, although a consensus appears to be building.

(1) Some courts will extend broad copyright protection to the structure, sequence, and organization of the program, in addition to the literal code of the program. *See* Whelan Associates, Inc. v. Jaslow Dental Laboratory, Inc., 797 F.2d 1222 (3d Cir. 1986), *cert. denied*, 479 U.S. 1031 (1987) (implying that a computer program can have only one idea).

(2) Other courts have taken the position that the structure, sequence, and organization of a computer program is an unprotectible idea. *See* Synercom Technology, Inc. v. University Computing Co., 462 F. Supp. 1003 (N.D. Tex. 1978) (analogizing the structure, sequence and organization to the H-shaped pattern of a manual transmission gear shift, finding both to be a nonprotectible idea); Plains Cotton Cooperative Ass'n v. Goodpasture Computer Services, Inc., 807 F.2d 1256 (5th Cir.), *cert. denied*, 484 U.S. 821 (1987). The Fifth Circuit has recently retreated somewhat from this approach in Kepner-Tregoe, Inc. v. Leadership Software, Inc., 29 U.S.P.Q.2d 1747 (5th Cir. 1994).

(3) Most of the courts addressing the copyrightability of the non-literal aspects, the structure, sequence and organization, of computer programs have adopted the "abstraction-filtration-comparison"

test set forth in Computer Associates International, Inc. v. Altai, Inc., 982 F.2d 693 (2d Cir. 1992). That decision took a middle ground position finding that the structure, sequence, and organization may be protectible if original elements remain after ideas, public domain material and *scene a faire* material has been distilled from the program. The Altai approach has been met with approval by several circuits. *See e.g.*, Atari Games Corp. v. Nintendo of America, Inc., 975 F.2d 832, 839 (Fed. Cir. 1992); Sega Enterprises Ltd. v. Accolade, Inc., 977 F.2d 1510, 1524-25 (9th Cir. 1993); Kepner-Tregoe, Inc. v. Leadership Software, Inc., 29 U.S.P.Q.2d 1747 (5th Cir. 1994); Gates Rubber Company v. Bando Chemical Industries, Ltd, 9 F.3d 823 (10th Cir. 1993). The *Altai* court devised a three part test:

(a) Abstraction: The computer program is dissected according to its varying levels of generality, often in a manner which parallels the typical development of a program. While the abstractions test will necessary vary from case-to-case and program-to-program, *see generally* Andrew H. Rosen, *Virtual Reality: Copyrightable Subject Matter and the Scope of Judicial Protection*, 33 Jurimetrics J. 35 (1992), a computer program can often be parsed into at least six levels of generally declining abstraction: (i) the main purpose, (ii) the program structure or architecture, (iii) modules, (iv) algorithms and data structures, (v) source code, and (vi) object code. *See* Gates Rubber Company v. Bando Chemical Industries, Ltd, 9 F.3d 823, 834-35 (10th Cir. 1993).

(b) Filtration: The court then filters out unprotectible elements: ideas, procedures, processes, systems, methods of operation, facts, public domain material, expression merged into an idea, scenes a faire and elements dictated by such external factors as hardware standards, mechanical specifications, software standards, compatibility requirements, target industry demands and computer industry programming practices. *See* Gates Rubber Company v. Bando Chemical Industries, Ltd, 9 F.3d 823, 836-38 (10th Cir. 1993).

(c) Comparison: The resulting core of protected elements in the plaintiff's program can now be compared to the allegedly infringing work.

d. Computer chips have been given *sui generis* protection by the Semiconductor Chip Protection Act of 1984, 17 U.S.C. §§ 901-14. The period of protection is 10 years. See generally Lee Hsu, *Reverse Engineering Under the Semiconductor Chip Protection Act: Complications for Standard of Infringement*, 5 Albany L. J. of Science & Technology 249 (1996).

e. The protectibility of graphic user interfaces (GUI) and computer screen displays is also a dynamic area of the law. The early video game cases viewed screen displays as audiovisual works separate from the underlying computer program. *See* Stern Electronics, Inc. v. Kaufman, 669 F.2d 852 (2d Cir. 1982). More recently, courts have protected screen displays as separate audiovisual works that may contain copyrightable elements and may be protected as compilations of terms and symbols. *See* Digital Communication Associates, Inc. v. Softklone Distributing Corp., 659 F. Supp. 449 (N.D. Ga. 1987).

(1) The three-step *Altai* test has been used to determine the protectibility of screen displays. *See* Apple Computer, Inc. v. Microsoft Corp., 35 F.3d 1435 (9th Cir. 1994) (court rejected Apple's claim of copyright protection for the "look and feel" of its screen displays, found Apple's use of a desktop metaphor, windowing and selected icons not protected by copyright, and held Microsoft's Windows screen display not virtually identical to Apple's compilation of screen elements). *See also* Engineering Dynamics, Inc. v. Structural Software, Inc., 26 F.3d 1335 (5th

Cir. 1994); Mitek Holdings, Inc. v. ArcE Engineering Co., Inc, 89 F.3d 1548 (11th Cir. 1996).

(2) The menu command hierarchy of Lotus' 1-2-3 spreadsheet program was held to be a "method of operation" that is not copyrightable under § 102(b). Lotus Development Corp. v. Borland International, Inc., 49 F.3d 807 (1st Cir. 1995), *aff'd by an equally divided Court*, 516 U.S. 233 (1996) *See also* Mitek Holdings, Inc. v. ArcE Engineering Co., Inc, 89 F.3d 1548 (11th Cir. 1996).

f. Reverse engineering is one topic which is beginning to attract the attention of the courts. The issue which arises is whether a competitor should be permitted to copy a computer program in an effort to decompile its object code as a means of obtaining the unprotected ideas contained in the code. Early cases took a strict view of this practice, see Hubco Data Products Corp. v. Management Assistance, Inc., 219 U.S.P.Q. 450 (D. Idaho 1983). More recent cases, emphasizing the need to ensure competition in the computer industry, have taken a more lenient view. *See* Sega Enterprises Ltd. v. Accolade, Inc., 977 F.2d 1510 (9th Cir. 1993). *But see* Sony Computer Entertainment Inc. v. Connectix Corp., 48 F. Supp. 2d 1212 (N.D. Cal. 1999) (intermediate copying of computer program to develop a substitute product, rather than to make own product compatible, not considered a fair use).

(1) The Digital Millennium Copyright Act permits circumvention of copyright protection systems as a step in reverse engineering necessary to achieve interoperability of an independently created computer program with other programs, to the extent such reverse engineering is otherwise permitted by copyright law. *See* 17 U.S.C. § 1201(f).

g. § 117 Limitations.

(1) Section 117 gives "the owner of a copy of a computer program" certain rights that constitute a lim-

itation on the exclusive rights contained in the copyright of the computer program.

(a) The Copyright Act does not define the term "owner" in this context. Case law differs as to its meaning. *Compare* MAI Sys. Corp. v. Peak Computer, Inc., 991 F.2d 511 (9th Cir. 1995) (licensee of computer program not an owner) *with* DSC Communications Corp. v. Pulse Communications, Inc., 170 F.3d 1354, 1361 (Fed. Cir. 1999) (licensee with severely limited contractual rights that are inconsistent with the rights normally enjoyed by owners of copies of software is not an owner).

(2) The 1976 Copyright Act provides for authorized copying by the owner of a computer program when it is an essential step in the utilization of the program in conjunction with the computer or when the copy is used for archival purposes. 17 U.S.C. § 117. *See* Allen-Myland, Inc. v. Int'l Business Machines Corp., 746 F. Supp. 520, 536 (E.D. Pa. 1990) (holding that § 117(1) permits copying of a program into RAM in order to permit the computer to execute the program).

(a) § 117 has been found not to protect a third-party maintenance firm that copied software from the hard drive into the computer's Random Access Memory (RAM). MAI Systems Corp. v. Peak Computer, Inc., 991 F.2d 511 (9th Cir. 1993).

i) The Digital Millennium Copyright Act permits the owner or lessee of a computer to authorize the making of a copy of a computer program through the activation of the computer hardware for purposes of machine maintenance or repair. *See* 17 U.S.C. § 117(c).

(3) The owner of a computer program is permitted to make an adaptation of the computer program, without authorization from the copyright owner,

as an essential step in the utilization of the computer program. 17 U.S.C. § 117. *See* Aymes v. Bonelli, 47 F.3d 23 (2d Cir. 1995) (adaptation permitted where changes necessary to keep program current and to maintain its viability with an upgraded computer system); Synergistic Technologies, Inc. v. IDB Mobile Communications, Inc., 871 F. Supp. 24 (D.D.C. 1994); Midway Mfg. Co. v. Strohon, 564 F. Supp. 741, 745 n.2 (N.D. Ill. 1983).

9. Typeface design.

   a. Though some typefaces may have sufficient originality to be copyrightable, Congress, as a matter of public policy, has determined that the design of typefaces will not be protected.

B. Musical works.

1. Undefined in the Copyright Act, musical works consist of music (melody, harmony, rhythm, etc.) and any accompanying words. *See* Mills Music, Inc. v. Arizona, 187 U.S.P.Q. 22 (D. Ariz. 1975), *aff'd per curiam*, 591 F.2d 1278 (9th Cir. 1979); Raphael Metzger, *Name That Tune: A Proposal for an Intrinsic Test of Musical Plagiarism*, 34 ASCAP Copr. Symp. 203 (1987).

2. When dealing with a recording of a musical composition, the underlying musical work should be distinguished from the sound recording of a performance of the musical work.

C. Dramatic works.

1. Undefined in the Copyright Act, dramatic works may include plays, screenplays, stage musicals and operas.

2. Dramatic musical works are not subject to compulsory mechanical license provisions of § 115. *See* Frank Music Corp. v. Metro-Goldwyn-Mayer, Inc., 772 F.2d 505 (9th Cir. 1985).

D. Pantomimes and choreographic works.

1. These works, undefined in the Copyright Act, are protected. 17 U.S.C. § 102(a)(4). The routine must rise to the level of

protectible expression. Horgan v. Macmillan, Inc., 789 F.2d 158 (2d Cir. 1986) (Balanchine Nutcracker).

E. Pictorial, graphic and sculptural works.

1. Maps.

a. Maps are pictorial works which often are compilations of facts. As such, the selection, coordination or arrangement of the elements forming the map are protectible, if sufficiently original. United States v. Hamilton, 583 F.2d 448 (9th Cir. 1978); Mason v. Montgomery Data, Inc., 967 F.2d 135 (5th Cir. 1992); Nester's Map & Guide Corp. v. Hagstrom Map Co., 796 F. Supp. 729 (E.D.N.Y. 1992). Earlier cases required that the author of a map engage in the "direct observation" of terrain features to obtain copyright protection. *See* Amsterdam v. Triangle Publications, 93 F. Supp. 79 (E.D. Pa. 1950), *aff'd on opinion below*, 189 F.2d 104 (3d Cir. 1951). This "sweat of the brow" approach has most likely been overruled by the Feist decision.

2. Colors are not protected by copyright.

a. Color, as an independent element, may not be protected by copyright. However, the distinctive selection, arrangement and layout of colors may be protected by copyright. Reader's Digest Ass'n v. Conservative Digest, Inc., 821 F.2d 800, 806 (D.C. Cir. 1987).

3. Useful Articles or Works of Applied Art.

a. Works of industrial design seeking protection as pictorial, graphic or sculptural works are precluded from copyright protection. Esquire v. Ringer, 591 F.2d 796 (D.C. Cir. 1979) (outdoor lighting fixture not protectible); Poe v. Missing Persons, 745 F.2d 1238 (9th Cir. 1984) (clothing not protectible); Brandir International, Inc. v. Cascade Pacific Lumber Co. , 834 F.2d 1142 (2d Cir. 1987) (bicycle rack not protectible).

(1) However, a protected pictorial, graphic or sculptural work may be reproduced in or on any kind

of article, whether useful or otherwise. 17 U.S.C. § 113(a). *See, e.g.*, Soptra Fabrics Corp. v. Stafford Knitting Mills, Inc., 490 F.2d 1092 (2d Cir. 1974) (fabric designs imprinted on material are protected by copyright); Eve of Milady v. Impression Bridal, Inc., 957 F. Supp. 484 (S.D.N.Y. 1997) (lace designs on bridal gown copyrightable).

b. Copyright law will not allow copyright protection of a pictorial, graphic or sculptural work which is deemed to be a useful article except to the extent that its design incorporates artistic features that can be identified separately from the functional elements of the articles. Where an article has both an ornamental function and a utilitarian function, copyright will protect the ornamental aspect of the article if it can be separated from the utilitarian aspect of the article. *See generally* Rebecca Ishaq Foster, *Protect the Bastard Child of the Arts: Copyright Protection for Theatrical Costumes*, 22 Sw. U. L. Rev. 431 (1993).

(1) Physical Separability.

(a) If copyrightable elements can be identified as physically separable from the utilitarian aspects of the article, then those elements will be protected. *See* Mazer v. Stein, 347 U.S. 201 (1954).

(b) For example, a two-dimensional painting, drawing or graphic work is still capable of being identified as such when it is printed on or applied to utilitarian articles such as textile fabrics, wallpaper, containers, and the like. A statue or carving which is used to embellish an industrial product or is incorporated into a product without losing its ability to exist independently as a work of art, continues to have copyright protection. *See* Mazer v. Stein, 347 U.S. 201 (1954).

(2) Conceptual Separability.

(a) If the copyrightable elements can be identified as conceptually separable from the utilitarian aspects of the article, then those elements will be protected. This notion is particularly important in the area of "conceptual art". There is currently a split of authority regarding the test of conceptual separability.

(b) One view holds that conceptual separability exists only if the artistic features of the article are superfluous or wholly unnecessary to performance of the utilitarian function. *See e.g.* Carol Barnhart, Inc. v. Economy Cover Corp., 773 F.2d 411 (2d Cir. 1985) (sculptures of human torsos sold as mannequins not copyrightable); *but see* Superior Form Builders v. Dan Chase Taxidermy, 74 F.3d 488 (4th Cir. 1996) (creating animal mannequins with body expressions was sufficient creative effort for copyright protection).

(c) Another view focuses on the intent of the author. *See* Brandir International, Inc. v. Cascade Pacific Lumber Co., 834 F.2d 1142 (2d Cir. 1987) (conceptual separability exists "where the design elements can be identified as reflecting the designer's artistic judgment exercised independently of functional influences").

(d) Another view holds that conceptual separability is determined by analyzing several factors, including (1) expert opinion concerning the usefulness of the work and whether any apparent functional aspects can be separated from the artistic aspects; (2) evidence of the author's intent in designing the work; (3) testimony concerning the custom and usage within the art world and the relevant trade concerning such objects; and (4) the marketability of the object as a work of art. After determining the extent of separable copyrightable elements, copyright protection will be afforded if the decorative or aesthetically pleasing aspect of the article is "primary" and the utilitarian function is "secondary". *See* Poe v. Missing Persons, 745 F.2d 1238 (9th Cir. 1984) (whether "Aquatint No. 5" constituted art as an artist's impression of an article of clothing or a useful article as a swimsuit is a question of fact); Ted Arnold Ltd. v. Silvercraft Co., 259 F. Supp. 733 (S.D.N.Y. 1966) (simulation antique telephone used for pencil sharpener held to be protectible); Kieselstein-Cord v. Accessories By Pearl, Inc., 632 F.2d 989 (2d Cir. 1980) (belt buckles found to be protectible sculptural works).

(3) Toy exception.

(a) Courts have tended to find toys not to be "useful articles," thereby bypassing the separability issue. *See e.g.*, Gay Toys, Inc. v. Buddy L. Corporation, 703 F.2d 970 (6th Cir. 1983); Masquerade Novelty, Inc. v. Unique Industries, Inc., 912 F.2d 663 (3d Cir. 1990) (nose masks); *see also* OddzOn Products, Inc. v. Oman, 924 F.2d 346, 350 (D.C. Cir. 1991); *but see* Whimsicality, Inc. v. Rubie's Costume Co., 891 F.2d 452 (2d Cir. 1989) (Halloween costume found to be noncopyrightable useful article).

c. Copyright law does not prevent the reproduction of the protected elements of useful articles in advertisements, commentaries or news reports. 17 U.S.C. § 113(c).

F. Audiovisual works.

1. An audiovisual work consists of a "series of related images which are intrinsically intended to be shown by the use of machines or devices . . . together with accompanying sounds. . . ." 17 U.S.C. § 101. While the images need not be presented serially, the images must be related to each other. *See* WGN Continental Broadcasting Co. v. United Video, Inc., 693 F.2d 622 (7th Cir. 1982).

2. The term "audiovisual work" should be broadly construed to enable courts to deal with new technologies or new adap-

tations of technologies. *See* Midway Manufacturing Co. v. Arctic International, Inc., 704 F.2d 1009, 1011 (7th Cir. 1982) (term "audiovisual work" should be broadly construed "to refer to any set of images displayed as some kind of unit.").

a. The audiovisual works category includes more than motion pictures and television programs. *See, e.g.*, Apple Computer, Inc. v. Microsoft Corp., 35 F.3d 1435 (9th Cir. 1994) (computer screen display); Stern Electronics, Inc. v. Kaufman, 669 F.2d 852 (2d Cir. 1982) (computer video game); Atari Games Corp. v. Oman, 979 F.2d 242 (D.C. Cir. 1992) (computer video game); Worlds of Wonder, Inc. v. Veritel Learning Systems, Inc., 658 F. Supp. 351, 354-55 (N.D. Tex. 1986) (animated plush toy bear).

3. The United States Copyright Office has decided to allow the copyright registration of "colorized" motion pictures. The Copyright Office determined that the selection and arrangement of colors through the use of modern technology which uses a pallet of 16 million colors constitutes sufficient originality for copyright protection.

G. Sound recordings.

1. Defined as the fixation of a series of musical, spoken, or other sounds.

2. The Copyright Act's definition of "sound recording" does not include the sounds accompanying a motion picture or other audiovisual work. A motion picture soundtrack is protected under the motion picture copyright. 17 U.S.C. § 101; Maljack Productions, Inc. v. Goodtimes Home Video Corp., 81 F.3d 881, 888 (9th Cir. 1996).

3. Pre-1972 sound recordings.

a. Sound recordings fixed prior to February 15, 1972, are not protected by federal copyright law. Such works may be protected, if at all, by state property, unfair competition, or criminal law.

(1) Any state statutory or common law protection of pre-1972 sound recordings will be preempted as of February 15, 2067. 17 U.S.C. § 301(c).

H. Architectural works.

1. Prior to December 1, 1990.

a. Most architectural works were deemed to be useful articles which could not be protected by copyright. Only non-utilitarian structures, such as monuments, could be protected.

b. Blueprints and drawings were protectible by copyright.

2. Architectural Protection Act of 1990 became effective December 1, 1990.

a. Structures may now be protected by copyright law. The Architectural Works Protection Act of 1990 created the new subject matter category of "architectural works." 17 U.S.C. § 102(a)(8). The useful article analysis, which is relevant only to the category of pictorial, graphic and sculptural works, is deemed not applicable to the architectural works category.

(1) An architectural work is defined as "the design of a building as embodied in any tangible medium of expression, including a building, architectural plans, or drawings." 17 U.S.C. § 101.

(a) A "building" is defined in the legislative history as any habitable structure, such as houses and office buildings, as well as structures that are used, but not inhabited by human beings, such as churches and gazebos.

(b) Copyright protection is not provided to nonhabitable structures such as interstate highway bridges, cloverleafs, canals, dams and pedestrian walkways.

b. Protection may be given to interior as well as exterior architectural elements. Protection is extended to individual original design elements and to the overall form of the building as well as the arrangement and composition of spaces and unprotectible elements in the design. 17 U.S.C. § 101.

(1) Sculpture that is incorporated into a building's structure is considered to be an architectural work. Leicester v. Warner Bros., 47 U.S.P.Q.2d 1501 (C.D. Cal. 1998).

c. Protection does not extend to individual standard features, such as common windows, doors, and other staple building components. 17 U.S.C. § 101.

(1) Elements determined by pragmatic, constructional and technical requirements are not protected.

(2) According to legislative history, functionality remains an issue as protection is accorded only when "the design elements are not functionally required."

(3) An original compilation of standard features may be protected.

(4) The Copyright Office is directed to register any structure which contains non-functional elements. The courts, rather than the Copyright Office, are to sort out the functional from the non-functional elements.

d. Limitations on protection.

(1) Notwithstanding the copyright in the structure, any person is permitted to make, distribute, or publicly display pictures, paintings, photographs, or other pictorial representations of the work, if the building is located in a public place or is ordinarily visible from a public place. 17 U.S.C. § 120(a). *See* Leicester v. Warner Bros., 47 U.S.P.Q.2d 1501 (C.D. Cal. 1998) (sculpture incorporated into an architectural work can be photographed by motion picture studio and used in feature film without a license).

(2) Notwithstanding the copyright in the structure, the owner of a building embodying an architectural

work may alter or destroy the building without the consent of the copyright owner. 17 U.S.C. § 120(b).

(3) State common law and statutes relating to "local landmarks, historic preservation, zoning or building codes" are not preempted. 17 U.S.C. § 301(b)(4).

e. Duration of protection.

(1) For architectural works created on or after December 1, 1990, the duration of protection is life of the author plus 70 years. In the case of works made for hire, anonymous or pseudonymous works, the duration of protection is the earliest date of 120 years from the creation of the work or 95 years from its first publication.

(2) For architectural works unconstructed on December 1, 1990, but embodied in unpublished plans or drawings, the duration of protection is life of the author plus 70 years, if the structure has been constructed by December 31, 2002. In the case of works made for hire, anonymous or pseudonymous works, the duration of protection is 120 years from the creation of the work, if the structure has been constructed by December 31, 2002. Protection will cease after December 31, 2002, if the structure is not constructed by that date. *See* Hunt v. Pasternack, 192 F.3d 877, 880 n.3 (9th Cir. 1999).

f. In addition to being protected as architectural works, architectural plans, drawings, and models continue to be protectible as pictorial, graphic, or sculptural works under § 102(a)(5). *See* Hunt v. Pasternack, 192 F.3d 877, 880 (9th Cir. 1999). The protection of an architectural work under § 102(a)(8) constitutes a separate copyright.

I. Derivative works.

1. A derivative work, a work which is based upon one or more preexisting works which are recast, transformed or adapted, is protected by an independent copyright. The copyright in

the derivative work extends only to the original new elements added by the author of the derivative work. 17 U.S.C. §§ 101, 103; G. Ricordi & Co. v. Paramount Pictures, Inc., 189 F.2d 469 (2d Cir.), *cert. denied*, 342 U.S. 849 (1951).

a. The Ninth Circuit requires that the new elements be sufficiently original to receive copyright protection, but does not require a work to be independently copyrightable in order for it to be considered a derivative work infringing on an underlying work. *See* Mirage Editions, Inc. v. Albuquerque A.R.T. Co., 856 F.2d 1341 (9th Cir. 1988), *cert. denied*, 489 U.S. 1018 (1989) (change of context, without reproduction, held to be sufficient transformation for creation of a derivative work); Lewis Galoob Toys, Inc. v. Nintendo of America, Inc., 964 F.2d 965, 967-69 (9th Cir. 1992).

2. Examples of derivative works include: translations, musical arrangements, art reproductions, editorial revisions, abridgments, dramatizations and fictionalizations. *See* Lamb v. Starks, 949 F. Supp. 753, 756 (N.D. Cal. 1996) (motion picture trailer is a derivative of the full-length movie); Marling v. Ellison, 218 U.S.P.Q. 702 (S.D.N.Y. 1982).

3. Mechanical translations lack sufficient originality for copyright protection. *See e.g.*, L. Batlin & Son, Inc. v. Snyder, 536 F.2d 486 (2d Cir. 1976) (en banc) (transforming an antique Uncle Sam bank into a new medium of a molded plastic replica held to contain insufficient originality); Entertainment Research Group, Inc. v. Genesis Creative Group, Inc., 122 F.3d 1211, 1222-23 (9th Cir. 1997) (differences in form, texture and proportionality between three-dimensional inflatable costumes and the two-dimensional cartoon characters on which they were based stemmed from unprotectible functional considerations); *but see* Alva Studios, Inc. v. Winniger, 177 F. Supp. 265 (S.D.N.Y. 1959) (exact scale reduction of Rodin's "Hand of God" held to contain sufficient originality for copyright protection).

4. A derivative work which has been based upon an underlying work, which is protected by copyright, without autho-

rization, may be denied copyright protection. *See* 17 U.S.C. § 103(a). If the new elements of the derivative work are divorceable from underlying work, they will be protected by copyright. If the new elements of the derivative work have melded into the underlying work and are not divorceable, those new elements will have no copyright protection.

J. Compilations.

1. A compilation, a work formed by the collection and assembling of preexisting materials or data, may be protected by copyright. The copyright in the compilation protects the selection, coordination or arrangement of the preexisting materials. 17 U.S.C. §§ 101, 103. Protection of these elements, however, constitutes a "thin" copyright, one which provides only limited protection. *See* Kregos v. Associated Press, 937 F.2d 700 (2d Cir. 1991). There are categories of compilations: collective works, factual compilations and non-factual compilations.

2. Collective works.

   a. A collective work is a collection of copyrightable materials which may or may not be independently protected by copyright. Examples include periodicals, anthologies and encyclopedias. 17 U.S.C. § 101. The copyright in the collective work extends only to the original selection, coordination or arrangement of separate and independent works included in the collective work. 17 U.S.C. § 103(b). The authors of the contributed works retain the copyright in their independent works. 17 U.S.C. § 201(c). *See* Quinto v. Legal Times of Washington, Inc., 506 F. Supp. 554 (D.D.C. 1981).

      (1) Publishers are authorized to reproduce an individual contribution to a collective work as part of any revision of the collective work in which it initially appeared. 17 U.S.C. § 201(c). *See* Tasini v. New York Times Co., 1999 WL 753966 (2d Cir. Sept. 24, 1999) (inclusion of articles, written by freelance

authors for newspapers and magazines, in electronic data bases and CD-ROM programs held not to be revisions of the collective works permitted by section 201(c)).

3. Compilations of informational matter.

   a. Works such as directories, databases, parts lists and other types of collected uncopyrightable data may be protected by copyright. The copyright protects only the selection, coordination or arrangement which is sufficiently original. *See* Feist Publications, Inc. v. Rural Telephone Service Company, Inc., 499 U.S. 340 (1991) (the vast majority of compilations are presumed to meet the minimal requirements of originality).

      (1) Creativity in the Selection of Information.

         (a) The more numerous and diverse the criteria applied to make the selection of material from the universe of relevant information, the greater the likelihood that the compilation will be deemed sufficiently original. *See* Matthew Bender & Co., Inc. v. West Publishing Co., 158 F.3d 674, 682 (2d Cir. 1998) ("creativity inheres in making non-obvious choices from among more than a few options").

         (b) The lower the percentage of material used from the universe of relevant information, the greater the likelihood that the compilation will be deemed sufficiently original. *See* Eckes v. Card Prices Update, 736 F.2d 859 (2d Cir. 1984) (choosing 5,000 premium cards out of a universe of 18,000 baseball cards constituted sufficient "selection" for copyright protection).

            i) Selection of the entire universe of relevant information lacks sufficient creativity to be protectible. *See, e.g.*, Warren Publishing, Inc. v. Microdos Data Corp., 115 F.3d 1509

(11th Cir. 1997) (publisher included all cable systems known to it in its factbook, which was held to have insufficient originality for copyright protection).

(2) Creativity in the arrangement of information.

(a) The greater the number of categories in which the information is arranged, the greater the likelihood that the compilation will be deemed sufficiently original. *See* Key Publications, Inc. v. Chinatown Today Publishing Enterprises, Inc., 945 F.2d 509 (2d Cir. 1991) (yellow pages directory which contained a unique organization of business listings and advertisements held to be protected by copyright).

(b) The use of obvious, garden-variety or routine categories in the arrangement of information will not be sufficiently original for protection. *See* Feist Publications, Inc. v. Rural Telephone Service Company, Inc., 499 U.S. 340 (1991); Bellsouth Advertising & Publishing Corporation v. Donnelly Information Publishing, Inc., 933 F.2d 952 (11th Cir. 1991) (arrangement and coordination of classified business directory contained insufficient originality).

(c) Creativity is lacking where the selection is dictated by industry conventions or other external factors, such that any person composing such a compilation would necessarily select the same categories of information. *See* Matthew Bender & Co., Inc. v. West Publishing Co., 158 F.3d 674, 682 (2d Cir. 1998); Mid America Title Co. v. Kirk, 59 F.3d 719, 722 (7th Cir. 1995); Victor Lalli Enters., Inc. v. Big Red Apple, Inc., 936 F.2d 671, 672 (2d Cir. 1991); Toro Co. v. R & R Products Co., 787 F.2d 1208 (8th Cir. 1986) (replacement part numbers used in sales catalogue not protectible).

(3) Neither Congress nor the courts have defined the elements of creativity in the coordination of information.

b. Earlier cases which, under the "sweat of the brow" theory, protected the compiler's industry and expense, rather than the compiler's selection, coordination or arrangement, have now been overruled by the Feist decision. "[C]opyright is not a tool by which a compilation author may keep others from using the facts or data he or she has collected." Feist Publications, Inc. v. Rural Telephone Service Company, Inc., 499 U.S. 340, 359 (1991). *See* Matthew Bender & Co., Inc. v. West Publ'g Co., 158 F.3d 693, 708 (2d Cir. 1998).

c. Individual recipes have been held not to be protected as compilations, but a book of recipes may be protected as a compilation protecting the selection, coordination and arrangement of the individual recipes. *See* Publications International, Ltd. v. Meredith Corp., 88 F.3d 473 (7th Cir. 1996).

d. Although earlier decisions had held that the volume and page numbers of case reporters were protected as part of the copyrighted compilation of judicial opinions, *see, e.g.*, West Publ'g Co. v. Mead Data Central, Inc., 799 F.2d 1219 (8th Cir. 1986), more recent decisions have found that the use by competitors of star paging indicating the page breaks in published court opinions does not constitute copyright infringement. *See, e.g.*, Matthew Bender & Co., Inc. v. West Publ'g Co., 158 F.3d 693 (2d Cir. 1998).

4. Non-Factual compilations.

a. The user interface of a computer program may be protected as a compilation. *See* Mitek Holdings, Inc. v. ArcE Engineering Co., Inc., 89 F.3d 1548 (11th Cir. 1996) (protection only against virtually identical compilation of elements); Apple Computer, Inc. v. Microsoft Corp., 35 F.3d 1435 (9th Cir. 1994).

b. The elements of an audiovisual work may be protected as a compilation. *See* Atari Games Corp. v. Oman, 888 F.2d 878 (D.C. Cir. 1989).

c. The elements of a radio broadcast, such as music and advertisements, may be protected as a compilation. *See* Infinity Broadcasting Corp. v. Kirkwood, 150 F.3d 104, 109 (2d Cir. 1998).

d. The elements of a magazine cover may be protected as a compilation. *See, e.g.*, Reader's Digest Ass'n v. Conservative Digest, Inc., 821 F.2d 800, 806 (D.C. Cir. 1987) ("Reader's Digest has combined and arranged common forms to create a unique graphic design and layout.").

e. A fictional graphic character may be protected as a compilation. *See, e.g.*, Lone Wolf McQuade Associates v. CBS, Inc., 961 F. Supp. 587 (S.D.N.Y. 1997) (character J.J. McQuade protected); Metro-Goldwyn-Mayer, Inc. v. American Honda Motor Co., Inc., 900 F. Supp. 1287 (C.D. Cal. 1995) (James Bond character as expressed in films protected).

K. Some works are not protectible by copyright even though they may be original to the author.

1. Government Works.

a. A work prepared by an officer or employee of the United States government as part of that person's official duties can not be protected by copyright. 17 U.S.C. § 105. *See* Matthew Bender & Co., Inc. v. West Publishing Co., 158 F.3d 674, 679 (2d Cir. 1998); Scherr v. Universal Match Corp., 417 F.2d 497 (2d Cir. 1969).

(1) The 1976 Copyright Act does not provide a specific prohibition against copyright protection for works prepared under federal government contract or grant. Each federal agency is permitted to determine whether it will withhold copyright protection, grant copyright protection, or consider the issue on

a contract-by-contract basis. Schnapper v. Foley, 667 F.2d 102 (D.C. Cir. 1981).

b. The § 105 prohibition does not affect the copyrightability of works created by employees of state governments.

c. If the work constitutes an "edict of government", whether federal or state, it can not be protected by copyright. A work is an edict of government if it constitutes a document of basic governmental action. *See* Wheaton v. Peters, 33 U.S. (8 Pet.) 591 (1834) (judicial opinions); Building Officials & Code Administrators International v. Code Technology, Inc., 628 F.2d 730 (1st Cir. 1980) (building code incorporated into state regulation, pursuant to license, now in public domain); Georgia v. Harrison Co., 548 F. Supp. 110 (N.D. Ga. 1982), *vacated by agreement between the parties*, 559 F. Supp. 37 (N.D. Ga. 1983) (codification of statutory law).

(1) Works merely referenced by government statutes or regulations are not deemed an edict of government. *See* CCC Information Services, Inc. v. MacLean Hunter Market Reports, Inc., 44 F.3d 61 (2d Cir. 1994); Practice Management Info. Corp. v. American Medical Ass'n, 121 F.3d 516, 518-20 (9th Cir. 1997).

IV. OWNERSHIP OF COPYRIGHT.

A. Distinction between the ownership of the copyright and the ownership of the material object.

1. The copyright in a work of authorship is distinct from the object in which it is fixed. The author owns the copyright in a literary work, the consumer owns the book which contains the literary work. The transfer of ownership of one does not necessarily transfer the ownership of the other. 17 U.S.C. § 202. *See* Salinger v. Random House, Inc., 811 F.2d 90 (2d Cir. 1987) (author retained copyright in letters he sent to friends).

2. The sole possible exception to this rule are works of fine art, protected by state common law copyright, which were

transferred prior to 1978, where the intent of the parties regarding the copyright in the work was unclear. *See* Pushman v. New York Graphic Society, Inc., 287 N.Y. 302, 39 N.E.2d 249 (1942). The "Pushman rule" was overruled by the New York legislature in 1966, the California legislature in 1976.

B. Works of individual authorship.

1. As a general rule, the author of a work is the party who actually creates the work, that is, the person who translates an idea into a fixed, tangible expression entitled to copyright protection. The copyright is owned by the author of the work. 17 U.S.C. § 201(a); Community for Creative Non-Violence v. Reid, 490 U.S. 730, 737 (1989).

C. Works Made For Hire. 17 U.S.C. § 201(b).

1. The "work for hire" doctrine holds that under certain employment conditions, the actual creator of a work is not the legal "author" of the work. When these conditions exist, the employer/buyer of the work is found to be the initial legal author of the work for copyright purposes, making the employer/buyer the sole owner of the copyright in the work from the time of its creation. Two situations present themselves in the work for hire area: works created by traditional employees and works created by independent contractors.

2. 1909 Act (works created pre-1978).

a. Under the 1909 Copyright Act, the party at whose "instance and expense" a work was created was presumed to be its legal "author" for copyright purposes. Dolman v. Agee, 157 F.3d 708, 712 (9th Cir. 1998); Playboy Enterprises, Inc. v. Dumas, 53 F.3d 549 (2d Cir. 1995).

(1) Evidence that a work was created at the "instance" of a party includes whether the party was the motivating factor in producing the work and whether the party had the right to direct and supervise the production of the work. Playboy Enterprises, Inc. v. Dumas, 53 F.3d 549 (2d Cir. 1995).

(2) The presumption that the hiring party was the copyright owner could be overcome with evidence of a contrary agreement between the parties. Dolman v. Agee, 157 F.3d 708, 712 (9th Cir. 1998); Playboy Enterprises, Inc. v. Dumas, 53 F.3d 549 (2d Cir. 1995).

b. This was true whether the actual creator was an employee or an independent contractor. *See* Murray v. Gelderman, 566 F.2d 1307 (5th Cir. 1978); Easter Seal Society for Crippled Children and Adults of Louisiana, Inc. v. Playboy Enterprises, 815 F.2d 324, 325-27 (5th Cir. 1987); Picture Music, Inc. v. Bourne, Inc., 457 F.2d 1213 (2d Cir.), *cert. denied*, 409 U.S. 997 (1972). Determinations of authorship under the 1909 Act continue to be of importance. *See* Philadelphia Orchestra Assoc. v. Walt Disney Co.,821 F. Supp. 341 (E.D. Pa. 1993) (orchestra's recording of the soundtrack music for "Fantasia" was a work made for hire, therefore the orchestra had no right to royalties for sales of the motion picture in videocassettes and laser discs).

3. 1976 Act (works created on or after 1-1-78).

a. The 1976 Copyright Act clearly distinguishes between the creation of employees acting within the scope of their employment and the creation of independent contractors. The copyright in the creations of employees is presumed to be owned by the employer. The copyright in the creations of independent contractors is presumed to remain with the independent contractor. The changes made by the 1976 Copyright Act regarding works made for hire do not apply to works created before January 1, 1978. Roth v. Pritikin, 710 F.2d 934, 938-39 (2d Cir. 1983) (work for hire rules of the 1976 Copyright Act are applied prospectively, not retroactively).

b. Employees.

(1) Whether an individual creator is deemed to be an employee is determined by using a test which has been developed under the law of agency. The law

looks to various factors to determine whether the author was an employee of the hiring party. These factors include the hiring party's right to control the manner and means by which the work is created; the skill required to create the work; the source of the instruments or tools used to create the work; the location of the work; the duration of the relationship between the parties; whether the hiring party has the right to assign additional projects to the hired party; the extent of the hired party's discretion over when and how long to work; the method of payment; the hired party's role in hiring and paying assistants; whether the hiring party is in business; whether the work is part of the regular business of the hiring party; the provision of employee benefits; and the tax treatment of the hired party. Community For Creative Non-Violence v. Reid, 490 U.S. 730, 751-52 (1989). *See, e.g.*, Quintanilla v. Texas Television Inc., 139 F.3d 494, 497-98 (5th Cir. 1998) (concert producer was not the author of audiovisual work created by television crew permitted to videotape concert); Saenger Organization, Inc. v. Nationwide Ins. Licensing Assoc., Inc., 119 F.3d 55, 60-62 (1st Cir. 1997).

(a) The Reid test for employee status applies retroactively to all works created on or after January 1, 1978. Autoskill, Inc. v. National Educational Support Systems, Inc., 994 F.2d 1476 (10th Cir. 1993).

(b) While the Supreme Court in Reid established that no one factor was dispositive, subsequent decisions have found that the factors should be weighed according to their significance in the case. *See, e.g.*, Aymes v. Bonelli, 980 F.2d 857 (2d Cir. 1992) (greater weight given to certain Reid factors: "(i) the hiring party's right to control the manner and means of creation; (ii) the skill required; (iii) the provision of employee benefits; (iv) the tax treatment of the hired party; and (v) whether the hiring party had the right to assign additional projects to the hired party.").

(c) The hired party has been found to be an independent contractor where the hiring party failed to extend benefits or pay social security taxes. *See, e.g.*, MacLean Assocs., Inc. v. Wm. M. Mercer-Meidinger-Hansen, Inc., 952 F.2d 769 (3d Cir. 1991); Marco v. Accent Publishing Co., 969 F.2d 1547 (3d Cir. 1992).

(d) Works created by an officer of a corporation in the course and scope of her employment are considered to be works made for hire. *See* Lulirama Ltd, Inc. v. Axcess Broadcast Services, Inc., 128 F.3d 872, 875 n.1 (5th Cir. 1997).

(2) Assuming the creator of a work is found to be an employee, it must be determined whether the actual process of creating the work is within the employee's scope of employment. If it is found that the employee had created the work while working within the scope of her employment, the copyright in the work initially resides with the employer as a matter of law. 17 U.S.C. §§ 101, 201(b).

(a) Factors used in determining the scope of employment include whether the creation of the work is within the employee's job description, whether the work is of a type traditionally created by a person in the employee's position, whether it was created during official hours, on the employer's premises, using the employer's equipment, with the aid of the employer's support personnel, or using information available to the employee as part of the employee's employment and whether the work was related to the employer's projects. *See* Scherr v. Universal Match Corp., 417 F.2d 497, 500-01 (2d Cir.

1969), *cert. denied*, 397 U.S. 936 (1970); Food Lion, Inc. v. Capital Cities/ABC, Inc., 946 F. Supp. 420 (M.D. N.C. 1996), *aff'd*, 116 F.3d 472 (4th Cir, 1997) (undercover videotapes made by reporters while employed by grocery store were made outside the scope of employment and, therefore, did not constitute works made for hire); *but see* Miller v. CP Chemicals, Inc., 808 F. Supp. 1238 (D.S.C. 1992) (computer program created by employee at home, on the employee's own computer, on the employee's own time and without extra pay deemed within the scope of employment).

(b) The Restatement of Agency states that a servant's conduct is within the scope of employment "only if: (a) it is of the kind he is employed to perform; (b) it occurs substantially within the authorized time and space limits; [and] (c) it is actuated, at least in part, by a purpose to serve the master." Restatement (Second) of Agency §228 (1958); Avtec Systems, Inc. v. Peiffer, 21 F.3d 568, 571 (4th Cir. 1994).

(3) If the work was created while the employee was working outside the scope of her employment, the employee may be treated as an independent contractor if the work was specially ordered or commissioned. If not specially ordered or commissioned, the work is considered to be one of individual authorship. The mere fact that the creator of a work happens to be an employee does not allow the employer to claim authorship of every work created by the employee. "[N]o one sells or mortgages all the products of his brain to his employer by the mere fact of employment." Public Affairs Assocs. v. Rickover, 177 F. Supp. 601, 604-05 (D.D.C. 1959), *rev'd on other grounds*, 284 F.2d 262 (1960), *vacated for insufficient record*, 369 U.S. 111 (1962), *on remand*, 268 F. Supp. 444 (D.D.C. 1967).

(4) The parties may agree to change the ownership of the copyright pursuant to a written agreement signed by them. 17 U.S.C. § 201(b). It is not clear whether such a writing changes the initial status of the work or merely acts as a transfer of ownership. *See* Respect Inc. v. Committee on the Status of Women, 821 F. Supp. 531 (N.D. Ill. 1993).

c. Independent contractors.

(1) The 1976 Copyright Act fundamentally changed the application of the work for hire doctrine to the creations of independent contractors.

(2) The copyright in any "specially ordered or commissioned" work created by an independent contractor on or after January 1, 1978, is presumed to be owned by the independent contractor.

(a) Whether a work has been "specially ordered or commissioned" raises the same issue as to whether a work under the 1909 Act had been created at the "instance and expense" of the hiring party. Playboy Enterprises, Inc. v. Dumas, 53 F.3d 549 (2d Cir. 1995).

(3) This presumption may be overcome only by a written agreement, and then only if the work falls within the nine categories of specially commissioned works that can be works made for hire prescribed by the statute.

(a) In order for the commissioning party to be deemed the sole legal author of the commissioned work there must be a written agreement, signed by both parties, which specifies that the particular work is to be created as a "work made for hire." 17 U.S.C. § 101; Quintanilla v. Texas Television Inc., 139 F.3d 494, 497 (5th Cir. 1998); BPI Systems, Inc. v. Leith, 532 F. Supp. 208, 210 (W.D. Tex. 1981). *See* Playboy Enterprises, Inc. v. Dumas, 960 F. Supp. 710 (S.D.N.Y. 1997) (endorsement of checks by artist's business manager or accountants did not bind artist to work for hire agreement).

i) Although the Act does not specify that any particular language be used, the writing must mention a work-for-hire relationship. Playboy Enterprises, Inc. v. Dumas, 53 F.3d 549, 560 (2d Cir. 1995). *But see* Armento v. Laser Image, Inc., 950 F. Supp. 719, 731 (W.D.N.C. 1996) (copyright statute does not demand that specific words "work made for hire" appear in the writing).

ii) While an informal memorandum might suffice, there exists a split of authority as to when the writing must be signed. One line of authority requires that the writing be signed prior to the creation of the work at issue. *See* Schiller & Schmidt, Inc. v. Nordisco Corp., 969 F.2d 410, 413 (7th Cir. 1992); 1 P. Goldstein, Copyright: Principles, Law and Practice 404 (1989); W. Patry, Latman's The Copyright Law 120 (6th ed. 1986). Another line of authority permits a subsequent writing to confirm a prior oral agreement. *See* Magnuson v. Video Yesteryear, 85 F.3d 1424 (9th Cir. 1996); Playboy Enterprises, Inc. v. Dumas, 53 F.3d 549 (2d Cir. 1995).

(b) The work must fall into one of the explicit categories of works set forth in the Copyright Act which, when prepared as a specially ordered or commissioned work, may constitute a work for hire. Those statutory categories are: works specially ordered or commissioned for use (1) as a contribution to a collective work, (2) as part of a motion picture or other audiovisual work, (3) as a translation, (4) as a compilation, (5) as an instructional text, (6) as a test, (7) as answer material for a test, (8) as an atlas, or (9) as a supplementary work. In 1999, "sound recording" was added to the statutory categories.

i) Note that such works as photographs, computer programs and musical compositions are not included in these categories. *See* Lulirama Ltd, Inc. v. Axcess Broadcast Services, Inc., 128 F.3d 872 (5th Cir. 1997) (decision prior to the 1999 amendment found musical compositions and sound recordings did not fall within the statutory categories).

ii) An unresolved issue concerns whether a work, such as a photograph, which is used in the packaging of merchandise can be viewed as a contribution to a collective work which brings it within the statutory categories.

(c) If one or both of these requirements are not met, the independent contractor is deemed to be not only the author of the work, but the owner of its copyright as well. *See* Playboy Enterprises, Inc. v. Dumas, 53 F.3d 549 (2d Cir. 1995).

(d) Even though the commissioning party may not own the copyright, it will most likely be deemed to have an implied nonexclusive license to use the work in the manner contemplated by the parties at the time they entered into the agreement regarding the commissioned work. *See* Effects Associates, Inc. v. Cohen, 908 F.2d 555 (1990).

D. Joint Works.

1. The 1976 Copyright Act defines a joint work as one where (1) the authors collaborate with each other in creating the work; or (2) each of the authors prepared his or her contribution with the intention that it would be merged with the contributions of other authors as "inseparable [e.g. as in a novel or painting] or interdependent [e.g. as in words and music of a song] parts of a unitary whole." 17 U.S.C. § 101.

a. Intent to contribute to a joint work.

(1) The authors must intend at the time of the creation of the component materials to create a joint work. Each author must intend her contribution to constitute a part of a total work to which another will make or has made a contribution. As long as this intent is present, the authors need not even know one another. Edward B. Marks Music Corp. v. Jerry Vogel Music Co., 140 F.2d 266 (2d Cir. 1944). *See* Weissmann v. Freeman, 868 F.2d 1313 (2d Cir. 1989); Systems XIX, Inc. v. Parker, 30 F. Supp. 2d 1225, 1229 (N.D. Cal. 1998).

(2) A majority of courts have adopted a more stringent requirement that the putative joint authors mutually intended that each be a co-author at the time the work was created. *See* Childress v. Taylor, 945 F.2d 500 (2d Cir. 1991).

(a) This view emphasizes the existence of a contractual agreement by the participants or the identification as co-authors through billing or credit. *See* Thomson v. Larson, 147 F.3d 195, 201-02 (2d Cir. 1998) (evidence demonstrated that playwright did not intend for dramaturg to be co-author of the musical "Rent"); Childress v. Taylor, 945 F.2d 500 (2d Cir. 1991); BTE v. Bonnecaze, 43 F. Supp. 2d 619, 624-25 (E.D. La. 1999) (factors to determine co-authorship status are: "(i) the contributor's decision making authority over what changes are made and what is included in a work, (ii) the way in which the parties bill or credit themselves with regard to the work, (iii) any written agreements with third parties, and (iv) any other additional evidence.").

(b) Even a significant contribution to the work by the alleged co-author does not automatically suffice to confer co-authorship status on that contributor. Thomson v. Larson, 147 F.3d 195, 202 (2d Cir. 1998).

(c) Some courts have refused to apply the Childress heightened subjective intent test where the putative joint author occupies a traditional authorship role. *See, e.g.*, Systems XIX, Inc. v. Parker, 30 F. Supp. 2d 1225, 1228-29 (N.D. Cal. 1998) (Congress has explicitly recognized the potential joint authorship roles of producer and recording artist).

(3) Some courts look to the custom of the relevant industry or profession to determine the existence of co-authorship. *See, e.g.*, Words & Data, Inc. v. GTE Communications, Inc., 765 F. Supp. 570 (W.D. Mo. 1991); Systems XIX, Inc. v. Parker, 30 F. Supp. 2d 1225, 1228-29 (N.D. Cal. 1998).

(4) If the intent to merge occurs after the initial creation, the resulting work will be either a derivative work or a collective work.

b. Contribution to the joint work.

(1) Each co-author need not contribute equal amounts of authorship. For a person to be considered a co-author, however, her contribution must be more than de minimis (e.g. more than a word or a line to a song) and cannot be merely a financial contribution.

(2) A split of authority exists as to whether each author's contribution must be independently copyrightable, or whether the contribution of ideas may suffice.

(a) The majority view requires that the contribution of each joint author be copyrightable. *See* Erickson v. Trinity Theatre, Inc., 13 F.3d 1061 (7th Cir. 1994) (actors participating in improvisational scenes did not provide independently copyrightable expression and were held not to be joint authors); S.O.S., Inc. v. Payday, Inc.,

886 F.2d 1081, 1087 (9th Cir. 1989); 1 Paul Goldstein, Copyright: Principles, Law and Practice § 4.1.2 (1989).

i) The contribution must be fixed. *See* BTE v. Bonnecaze, 43 F. Supp. 2d 619, 624-25 (E.D. La. 1999) (band member was denied joint authorship status for musical compositions because his recording of the musical compositions did not serve as the fixation of his contributions to the musical composition).

(b) The minority view would permit joint author status for the contribution of ideas, so long as the resulting joint work has sufficient original expression. *See* 1 Melville Nimmer & David Nimmer, Nimmer on Copyright § 6.03 (1992).

2. In the case of a "joint work" the co-authors are co-owners of the copyright in the work. 17 U.S.C. § 201(a). Each contributor automatically acquires an undivided ownership in the entire work. Unless there is an agreement to the contrary, each co-owner has the independent right to use the work or to license non-owners to use the work. *See* Oddo v. Ries, 743 F.2d 630, 633 (9th Cir. 1984); *See* Werbungs und Commerz Union Austalt v. LeShufy, 6 U.S.P.Q.2d 1153 (S.D.N.Y. 1987). All authors share equally in the ownership of the joint work as tenants in common. The heirs of each author acquire her share of the joint work. A joint owner may transfer her interest in the work to a third party, but not the interest of any other joint owner without the latter's consent. The transferee stands in the shoes of the transferor. As a result, a single joint owner may not grant an exclusive license.

3. A joint owner must abide by the rule of mutual accountability. A joint owner is under a duty to account to other joint owners of the work for a prorateable share of profits realized from the use or licensing of the work. The right of accounting may be enforced only as against the

joint owner-licensor, not against the licensee. Oddo v. Ries, 743 F.2d 630, 633 (9th Cir. 1984) (duty to account is derived from general principles of law governing the rights of co-owners).

4. One joint owner cannot be liable for copyright infringement to another joint owner of the work. Richmond v. Weiner, 353 F.2d 41 (9th Cir. 1965); Donna v. Dodd, Mead & Co., Inc., 374 F. Supp. 429 (S.D.N.Y. 1974).

E. Joint Ownership.

1. Creation of a joint work is only one method of creating co-ownership of a work. Other methods include transferring or willing the copyright to more than one person, or through state community property laws. *See* In re Marriage of Worth, 195 Cal. App. 3d 768, 241 Cal. Rptr. 135 (1987) (non-authoring spouse is joint owner of copyright in any work created by authoring spouse during the marriage); Debora Polacheck, *The "Un-Worthy" Decision: The Characterization of a Copyright as Community Property*, 17 Comm/Ent 601 (1995). *But see* Rodrigue v. Rodrigue, 50 U.S.P.Q.2d 1278 (E.D. La. 1999) (community property law is preempted when it permits copyright ownership to vest in anyone other than the author); Edward R. Bernett, *In Search of Uniformity—State Marital Property Laws and the 'Balkinization' of Federal Copyright Ownership*, 24 NEW MATTER 1 (Sum. 1999).

2. When the copyright is owned by a partnership, each partner is a co-owner of the copyright. *See* Oddo v. Ries, 743 F.2d 630, 632 (9th Cir. 1984).

F. Divisibility of Copyright Ownership.

1. Under the 1976 Copyright Act, a copyright is divisible. A copyright is now viewed as a bundle of exclusive rights. Any of the § 106 exclusive rights that make up a copyright and any subdivision of them, can be transferred and owned separately, whether or not the transfer is limited in time, media or geographic area. 17 U.S.C. § 201(d). *See* Gamma Audio & Video, Inc. v. Ean-Chea, 11 F.3d 1106 (1st Cir. 1993).

G. Transfer of Copyright Ownership.

1. Any transfer of statutory copyright ownership (assignment or exclusive license), other than by operation of law, must be in writing and signed by the owner of the rights conveyed or her authorized agent. 17 U.S.C. § 204; Effects Associates, Inc. v. Cohen, 908 F.2d 555 (9th Cir. 1990) (producer's argument that moviemakers do lunch, not contracts, was insufficient to make an oral agreement an exclusive license); Papa's-June Music, Inc. v. McLean, 921 F. Supp. 1154, 1158 (S.D.N.Y. 1996) (writing requirement of § 204 applicable to transfers between joint authors).

   a. A growing number of circuits hold that under some circumstances a prior oral grant that is confirmed by a later writing becomes valid as of the time of the oral grant. *See* Magnuson v. Video Yesteryear, 85 F.3d 1424, 1428-29 (9th Cir. 1996); Arthur Rutenberg Homes, Inc. v. Drew Homes, Inc., 29 F.3d 1529 (11th Cir. 1994); Eden Toys, Inc. v. Florelee Undergarment Co., 697 F.2d 27, 36 (2d Cir. 1982).

   b. An exchange of e-mails does not satisfy the writing requirement of § 204. *See* Ballas v. Tedesco, 41 F. Supp. 2d 531, 541 (D.N.J. 1999).

2. In the case of a transfer of copyright ownership in a motion picture that is produced subject to one or more collective bargaining agreements, the transfer instrument is deemed to incorporate the assumption agreements applicable to the copyright ownership being transferred that are required by the applicable collective bargaining agreement. The transferee is subject to the obligations under the assumption agreement to make residual payments and provide related notices if the transferee knows or has reason to know that the collective bargaining agreement is applicable to the motion picture. 28 U.S.C. § 4001.

   a. The knowledge requirement is met through:

      (1) Actual knowledge; or

(2) Constructive knowledge arising from recordation with the Copyright Office or publication at an on-line site operated by the relevant union; or

(3) Awareness of other facts and circumstances pertaining to a particular transfer from which it is apparent that the collective bargaining agreement was or will be applicable to the motion picture.

b. Grants of Security Interests are Excluded.

3. Nonexclusive Licenses.

a. A nonexclusive license may be granted orally or implied from conduct. I.A.E., Inc. v. Shaver, 74 F.3d 768 (7th Cir. 1996); Effects Associates, Inc. v. Cohen, 908 F.2d 555 (9th Cir. 1990); Gracen v. Bradford Exchange, 698 F.2d 300 (7th Cir. 1983); Maxwell v. Veeck, 110 F.3d 749 (11th Cir. 1997); Systems XIX, Inc. v. Parker, 30 F. Supp. 2d 1225, 1230 (N.D. Cal. 1998) ("Permission to employ pre-existing copyrighted material in a sound recording need not be in writing, but can be granted orally or implied from conduct in the form of a non-exclusive license."). *But see* Johnson v. Jones, 149 F.3d 494, 500 (6th Cir. 1998) (almost every objective fact pointed away from existence of implied license).

(1) The copyright in a work created pursuant to an invalid work for hire agreement is owned by the independent contractor who created the work, but the hiring party retains a nonexclusive license. *See* Lulirama Ltd, Inc. v. Axcess Broadcast Services, Inc., 128 F.3d 872 (5th Cir. 1997).

b. The parameters of an implied nonexclusive license are determined by the intent of the parties at the time the agreement was entered into. *See* Effects Associates, Inc. v. Cohen, 908 F.2d 555 (9th Cir. 1990).

c. A nonexclusive license may be limited in scope. *See, e.g.,* Micro Star v. Formgen, Inc., 154 F.3d 1107, 1113 (9th Cir. 1998) (permission granted users of "Duke Nukem 3D" to create and distribute new levels of computer game maps on the condition they "must be offered solely for free" did not permit their use in a commercial product).

4. Grant of rights.

    a. While it is not required that the grant of rights explicitly mention "copyright" or "exclusive rights," *see* Schiller & Schmidt, Inc v. Nordisco Corp., 969 F.2d 410, 413 (7th Cir. 1992), the better practice is that it should. Papa's-June Music, Inc. v. McLean, 921 F. Supp. 1154, 1159 (S.D.N.Y. 1996); *cf.* Playboy Enterprises, Inc. v. Dumas, 53 F.3d 549, 564 (2d Cir. 1995) (writing that did not expressly mention copyright failed to meet requirements of section 204(a)).

        (1) Some courts are more demanding in their requirements that an assignment of copyright include use of such explicit terms. *See, e.g.*, Saxon v. Blann, 968 F.2d 676, 680 (8th Cir. 1992) ("the conveyance of 'ownership rights' to a book will not convey the copyright of the book. To transfer ownership of a copyright, the parties must state in writing that they intend to transfer a copyright.").

    b. There is a general presumption against the conveyance of renewal rights. *See* Corcovado Music Corp. v. Hollis Music, Inc., 981 F.2d 679, 684 (2d Cir. 1993).

        (1) This presumption may be rebutted where the grant includes language that expressly grants rights in "renewals of copyright" or "extensions of copyright." P.C. Films Corp. v. MGM/UA Home Video Inc., 138 F.3d 453, 457 (2d Cir. 1998).

        (2) General words of assignment can include renewal rights if the parties had so intended. Siegel v. National Periodical Pubs., Inc., 508 F.2d 909, 913 (2d Cir. 1974). *See* P.C. Films Corp. v. MGM/UA Home Video Inc., 138 F.3d 453, 457 (2d Cir. 1998) (grant of "perpetual and exclusive right to distribute" included renewal rights).

(a) The intention to convey renewal rights may be supported by extrinsic evidence. *See, e.g.*, Venus Music Corp. v. Mills Music, Inc., 261 F.2d 577, 578-79 (2d Cir. 1958).

(3) Where a contract is silent as to the duration of the grant of copyright rights, the contract is read to convey right for the initial copyright term only. P.C. Films Corp. v. MGM/UA Home Video Inc., 138 F.3d 453, 458 (2d Cir. 1998).

c. Where contractual language is ambiguous, courts will often look at the circumstances surrounding the agreement in an attempt to identify the intent of the parties regarding copyright ownership. The contract may be clarified by resort to parol evidence including the negotiations leading to the agreement, prior or subsequent dealings between the parties and evidence of the custom and practice of the industry involved. *See* Friedman v. Stacey Data Processing Servs., Inc., 17 U.S.P.Q.2d 1858, 1862 (N.D. Ill. 1990).

(1) Where the contractual language of a purported transfer of copyright ownership is deemed ambiguous, the author is generally favored in the analysis. *See* Pamfiloff v. Giant Records, Inc., 794 F. Supp. 933, 937 (N.D. Cal. 1992) ("we understand the policy underlying Section 204(a) to be tipped somewhat in favor of the original holder of the copyrighted material").

5. Recordation of transfers of copyright ownership.

a. Any "document pertaining to a copyright" may be recorded if it bears the actual signature of the person who executed it or is accompanied by a sworn or official certification that it is a true copy. 17 U.S.C. § 205.

b. In the case of conflicting transfers, the first good faith recorded transfer of a registered copyright is given priority unless an earlier transfer is recorded within one month after the earlier transfer's execution in the United States or two months after its execution outside the United States. 17 U.S.C. § 205(d).

c. The Copyright Act preempts the Uniform Commercial Code regarding the security interests in copyrighted works. In re Peregrine Entertainment Ltd., 116 B.R. 194 (C.D. Cal. 1990). Registration with the Copyright Office is a necessary precondition to filing the security interest with the Copyright Office in order to perfect the security interest. In re AEG Acquisition Corp., 127 B.R. 34 (C.D. Cal. 1991), *aff'd*, 161 B.R. 50 (9th Cir. 1993).

d. Assignment of right to receive royalties was not a transfer of copyright, therefore assignee was not required to record assignment to have priority over a subsequent IRS tax lien against assignor. Broadcast Music, Inc. v. Hirsch, 104 F.3d 1163 (9th Cir. 1997).

6. "New uses" of licensed works.

a. Where novel technological developments generate unforeseen applications for a previously licensed work, the scope of the license must be determined. See generally Michael R. Fuller, *Hollywood Goes Interactive: Licensing Problems Associated with Re-Purposing Motion Pictures into Interactive Multimedia Videogames*, 15 Loy. L.A. Ent. L.J. 599 (1995).

b. In the absence of evidence of the specific intent of the parties, a court will attempt to identify any indicia of a mutual general intent to apportion rights to "new uses." These indicia may be discerned from the language of the license, the surrounding circumstances and trade usage. Rey v. Lafferty, 990 F.2d 1379 (1st Cir. 1993).

c. Where no reliable indicia of general intent are discernible, the courts are divided on how to resolve the issue on policy grounds.

(1) Some courts, adopting an expansive view, will place the burden on the grantor to negotiate an exception where the possibility of non-specific "new uses" was foreseeable by the contracting parties at the time the licensing agreement was drafted. *See, e.g.*, Bartsch v. Metro-Goldwyn Mayer, Inc., 391 F.2d 150, 155 (2d Cir.), *cert. denied*, 393 U.S. 826

(1968); ABKCO Music, Inc. v. Westminster Music, Ltd. 838 F. Supp. 153, 155 (S.D.N.Y. 1993), *aff'd*, 41 F.3d 1502 (2d Cir. 1994) (a license should include any uses which may be reasonably read to fall within the license's scope). This approach favors the grantee, which generally will assure a greater degree of distribution of the work to the public. *But see* Boosey & Hawkes Music Publishers, Ltd. v. Walt Disney Co., 145 F.3d 481, 487 (2d Cir. 1998) ("new-use analysis should rely on neutral principles of contract interpretation rather than solicitude for either party").

(2) Other courts assume that a license of rights in a given medium includes only such uses as fall within the unambiguous core meaning of the term, therefore, any rights not expressly granted are reserved to the copyright owner. *See, e.g.*, Cohen v. Paramount Pictures Corp., 845 F.2d 851, 854 (9th Cir. 1988); Tele-Pac, Inc. v. Grainger, 570 N.Y.S.2d 521, *appeal dismissed*, 580 N.Y.S.2d 201, 588 N.E.2d 99 (1991) (broadcast rights do not encompass videocassette film rights). *But see* Maljack Productions, Inc. v. Goodtimes Home Video Corp., 81 F.3d 881, 885 (9th Cir. 1996) (sufficiently broad grant of rights clause may encompass use in a new technology even though the contract did not contain a future technologies clause).

d. The use of broad language in the granting clause will benefit the grantee. *See, e.g.*, Rooney v. Columbia Pictures Industries, Inc., 538 F. Supp. 211 (S.D.N.Y.), *aff'd*, 714 F.2d 117 (2d Cir. 1982), *cert. denied*, 460 U.S. 1084 (1983) (license to exhibit films "by any present or future methods or means"); Platinum Record Co. v. Lucasfilm, Ltd., 566 F. Supp. 226, 227 (D.N.J. 1983) (synchronization license to perform a musical composition "perpetually throughout the world by any means or methods now or hereafter known").

e. The use of broad language in a reservation of rights clause will benefit the grantor. *See, e.g.*, Cohen v. Paramount Pictures Corp., 845 F.2d 851, 854 (9th Cir. 1988). *See also* Rey v. Lafferty, 990 F.2d 1379 (1st Cir. 1993) (reservation of rights implied from the situation of the parties and the "general tenor" of the agreement).

H. Foreign Authors (17 U.S.C. § 104).

1. Unpublished works.

Unpublished works may be protected by United States copyright law without regard to the nationality or domicile of the author.

2. Published works.

Published works may be protected by United States copyright law under any one of the following conditions:

a. The author is a national or domiciliary of the United States or of a treaty party, or is a stateless person;

b. The work is first published in the United States or in a foreign nation that, on the date of first publication, is a treaty party;

c. The work is a sound recording that was first fixed in a treaty party;

d. The work is a pictorial, graphic, or sculptural work that is incorporated in a building or other structure, or an architectural work that is embodied in a building and the building or structure is located in the United States or a treaty party;

e. The work is first published by the United Nations, by any of its specialized agencies, or by the Organization of American States;

f. The work is within the scope of a Presidential proclamation extending protection to works originating in a specified country which extends protection to United States works on substantially the same basis as to its own works.

3. Restoration of Copyright Under GATT.

   a. Uruguay Round Agreements Act (URAA) which implemented the General Agreement on Tariffs and Trade (GATT) that included the Trade Aspects of Intellectual Property Rights Agreement (TRIPS) and the World Trade Organization Agreement (WTO), was signed into law on December 8, 1994. 17 U.S.C. § 104A.

   b. Restoration of Copyrights.

      (1) Qualifications for restoration.

         (a) Author of work must be a national or domiciliary of an eligible country:

            i) Member of the Berne Convention; or

            ii) Member of the World Trade Organization; or

            iii) Nation adhering to the WIPO Copyright Treaty or WIPO Performances and Phonograms Treaty; or

            iv) Is subject to a United States Presidential Proclamation.

         (b) The work must not be in the public domain in the Source Country.

         (c) The work must have been published in an eligible country at least 30 days prior to any publication in the United States.

      (2) Effective date of the restoration is January 1, 1996.

         (a) On that date the restoration is automatic.

         (b) The restored copyright will be automatically vested in the author of the restored work or in the initial right holder according to the law of the Source country.

         (c) The copyright in the Restored Work can be immediately enforced upon the effective date.

(3) Duration of copyright in the Restored Work.

(a) The remainder of copyright that the work would have had in the United States, but for the loss of U.S. copyright.

(4) Special "Reliance Party" defense.

(a) "Reliance Party" qualifications:

i) Party must have used the Restored Work both before and after January 1, 1996; and

ii) Party must have made or acquired copies of the Restored Work before January 1, 1996;

iii) Party must have bought or acquired at any time an interest in a derivative work based upon the Restored Work; or

iv) Party must have otherwise acquired significant assets (multiple copyrights, bulk assignments, inventory) from another Reliance Party.

(b) Liability of a Reliance Party.

i) If no "Notice of Intent to Enforce" is filed by the owner of the Restored Work, Reliance Party is immune from liability.

ii) If a "Notice of Intent to Enforce" is filed with the U.S. Copyright Office or served on a specific Reliance Party, a 1 year grace period is created during which the reliance party is immune from liability.

a) Reliance Party may sell its existing inventory.

b) Reliance Party may continue to use an existing derivative work.

c) Reliance Party may not make new copies, create new inventory or create new derivative works.

iii) Reliance Party may continue to use a derivative work based upon the Restored Work after the grace period, subject to the payment of reasonable compensation. If the parties cannot agree, a federal court may set the compensation.

a) It appears that this provision does not apply to derivative works created in the United States.

(5) Remedies.

(a) Restored Work is entitled to all the remedies of the U.S. Copyright Statute.

(b) Statutory damages and attorneys fees may be available if the infringement began after the work was registered with the Copyright Office. *See* 17 U.S.C. §§ 104A(d)(1) & (2), 412.

4. International copyright considerations.

a. There is no international copyright.

(1) The United States is a signatory to the two leading multilateral copyright treaties: the Universal Copyright convention and the Berne Convention. These treaties do not provide direct copyright protection. Operating on the principle of "national treatment," the treaties provide that a qualifying foreign work will receive protection which is equal to or greater than the protection given to the signatory's own works.

b. Distribution or other uses of works outside the United States are protected, if at all, by the copyright law of individual countries.

c. United States copyright law has no extraterritorial effect.

(1) While it is well established that copyright laws do not have extraterritorial application, United States copyright laws apply to any infringing activity which occurs, even in part, in the United

States. GB Marketing USA, Inc. v. Gerolsteiner Brunnen GmbH & Co., 782 F. Supp. 763 (W.D.N.Y. 1991). *But see* Danjaq, S.A. v. MGM/UA Communications Co., 773 F. Supp. 194, 201 (C.D. Cal. 1991) (no contributory or vicarious liability may be found where the infringing activity does not occur in the United States).

(a) Damages flowing from the foreign exploitation of domestic acts of infringement may be recovered. *See* Los Angeles News Service v. Reuters Television Int'l, Limited, 149 F.3d 987, 990-92 (9th Cir. 1998); Update Art, Inc. v. Modiin Publ'g, Ltd., 843 F.2d 67, 73 (2d Cir. 1988).

(2) Allegation of mere domestic authorization of extraterritorial acts of infringement is insufficient to state claim under Copyright Act in light of general lack of extraterritorial effect of United States copyright laws. Subafilms, Ltd. v. MGM-Pathe Communications Co., 24 F.3d 1088 (9th Cir. 1994); *but see* Curb v. MCA Records, Inc., 898 F. Supp. 586, 595 (M.D. Tenn. 1995) (domestic violation of the authorization right is an infringement "whenever the authorizee has committed an act that would violate the copyright owner's § 106 rights.").

V. PROTECTION OF EXCLUSIVE RIGHTS (17 U.S.C. § 106).

A. Reproduction Right. 17 U.S.C. § 106(1).

1. The exclusive right to reproduce a work extends to every kind of copyrightable work.

2. This right is defined as the right to produce a material object in which the work is duplicated, transcribed or simulated in a fixed form. *See* Walt Disney Productions v. Filmation Associates, 628 F. Supp. 871 (C.D. Cal. 1986) (copying of Disney animation as part of an intermediate step in Filmation's development of a motion picture was held to constitute an infringement).

a. The copying of a computer program into the RAM memory of a computer has been found to constitute an infringing reproduction. *See* MAI Systems Corp. v. Peak Computer, Inc., 991 F.2d 511 (9th Cir. 1993); Advanced Computer Services of Michigan v. MAI Systems, Corp., 845 F. Supp. 356 (E.D. Va. 1994).

(1) The Digital Millennium Copyright Act partially overruled the MAI line of cases by allowing the owner or lessee of a computer to authorize the making of a copy of a computer program through the activation of the computer hardware for purposes of machine maintenance or repair. *See* 17 U.S.C. § 117(c).

3. A "synchronization right," the ability to use a work, generally a musical composition or sound recording, in the soundtrack of an audiovisual work, has been deemed part of the reproduction right. *See* Agee v. Paramount Communications, Inc., 59 F.3d 317 (2d Cir. 1995).

4. One who fixes the sounds or images of a live performance, without the consent of the performer, is subject to the same remedies as an infringer of copyright. 17 U.S.C. § 1101.

5. Limitations on the exclusive reproduction right.

a. Libraries and archives are specially privileged to make reproductions under certain circumstances. 17 U.S.C. § 108.

b. The owner of copyright in a collective work has the right to reproduce individual contributions as part of that particular collective work, any revision of that collective work, and any later collective work in the same series. 17 U.S.C. § 201(c). *See* Tasini v. New York Times Co., 1999 WL 753966, at *3-4 (2d Cir. Sept. 24, 1999).

c. A transmitting organization that has the right to transmit any work may make an "ephemeral recording," a single copy of a particular program that must be subsequently destroyed if not preserved for archival purposes. 17 U.S.C. § 112; Agee v. Paramount Communications, Inc., 59 F.3d 317 (2d Cir. 1995).

(1) Transmitting organizations are permitted to circumvent copy protection technologies to facilitate their § 112 rights if the copyright owner fails to make available the means to reproduce the copyrighted material in a timely manner. 17 U.S.C. § 112(a)(2).

d. A non-controlled musical composition may be reproduced without the consent of the copyright owner pursuant to a compulsory mechanical license. 17 U.S.C. § 115. Under this compulsory license the composition can be recorded, manufactured in phonorecords and sold to the public for its private use, as long as the statutory royalty of 7.1 cents per unit is paid to the copyright owner. Stylistic changes to the composition are permitted, as long as the composition is not perverted or distorted, nor the fundamental character of the work changed. *See* ABKCO Music, Inc. v. Stellar Records, Inc., 96 F.3d 60 (2d Cir. 1996) (karaoke CD-ROM did not fall within § 115's compulsory mechanical license).

(1) The Digital Performance Right in Sound Recordings Act of 1995 has created a compulsory mechanical license for "digital phonorecord delivery," the distribution of recorded musical compositions by digital transmissions.

(a) Currently, the amount of the license is the same as the traditional § 115 compulsory mechanical license. 17 U.S.C. § 115(c)(3)(A).

(b) Unlike the traditional § 115 compulsory mechanical license, the compulsory mechanical license for "digital phonorecord delivery" may include controlled compositions. 17 U.S.C. § 115(c)(3)(E).

e. The owner of a copy of a computer program is permitted to copy the program into the memory of her computer and to make a single archival copy. 17 U.S.C. § 117.

f. The Audio Home Recording Act of 1992 permits unauthorized audio recording for noncommercial use. 17 U.S.C. § 1008.

(1) Funds from the sale of digital audio recording devices and media are collected from manufacturers, importers and sellers, and disbursed to record companies, recording artists, musicians, vocalists, music publishers and songwriters. These funds are intended to offset any economic losses due to noncommercial audio recording.

(2) Source of collected funds:

(a) The manufacturer, importer or seller of a digital audio recording device must pay 2% of the wholesale price of the unit, but not less than $1 or more than $8 per unit. 17 U.S.C. § 1004.

i) The device must include SCMS technology that precludes serial copying. *See* Recording Industry Association of America v. Diamond Multimedia Systems Inc., 180 F.3d 1072 (9th Cir. 1999) (Rio portable music player held not required to employ a Serial Copyright Management System because player, which is not able to reproduce a digital music recording "directly" or "from a transmission," was not a digital audio recording device).

(b) The manufacturer, importer or seller of digital audio recording media must pay 3% of the wholesale price of each unit. 17 U.S.C. § 1004.

(3) Disbursement of collected funds:

(a) Sound recordings fund receives 66 2/3%. 17 U.S.C. § 1006.

i) 2 5/8% of the sound recordings fund is distributed to nonfeatured musicians.

ii) 1 3/8% of the sound recordings fund is distributed to nonfeatured vocalists.

iii) The remaining balance, 96%, is divided between featured recording artists and record companies.

a) Featured recording artists receive 40% of the remaining balance.

b) Record companies receive 60% of the remaining balance.

(b) Musical works fund receives 33 1/3%. 17 U.S.C. § 1006.

i) 50% of the musical works fund is distributed to music publishers.

ii) 50% of the musical works fund is distributed to songwriters.

B. Adaptation Right. 17 U.S.C. § 106(2).

1. The exclusive right to prepare derivative works extends to every kind of copyrightable work.

2. The copyright owner has the exclusive right to prepare a translation, musical arrangement, dramatization, abridgment, or motion picture version of the protected work. *See e.g.* Grove Press, Inc. v. Greenleaf Publishing Co., 247 F. Supp. 518 (E.D.N.Y. 1965).

3. A split of authority has developed regarding the issue of whether the new elements of a work must meet the originality requirements for the work to be considered a derivative work infringing on the underlying work. The Ninth Circuit has held that placing a work in a new context in which the work is "recast, transformed or adapted" is sufficient to infringe the adaptation right without a showing that the change contained sufficient originality. *See* Mirage Editions, Inc. v. Albuquerque A.R.T. Co., 856 F.2d 1341 (9th Cir. 1988), *cert. denied*, 489 U.S. 1018 (1989) (removing prints from a book, pasting them on tile and framing the print constitutes an infringement). *But see* Lee v. A.R.T.

Co., 125 F.3d 580 (7th Cir. 1997) (placing plaintiff's notecards onto ceramic tile constituted insufficient originality to be deemed the creation of unauthorized derivative works); Precious Moments, Inc. v. La Infantil, Inc., 971 F. Supp. 66 (D.P.R. 1997); C.M. Paula Co. v. Logan, 355 F. Supp. 189 (N.D. Tex. 1973) (placing the work in a new context must be sufficiently original to be protectible as a derivative work for such action to be found an infringement).

4. The Copyright Act gives the publishers of collective works the right to reproduce and distribute individual contributions as part of "any revision of that collective work." 17 U.S.C. § 201(c). *See* Tasini v. New York Times Co., 1999 WL 753966, at *3-4 (2d Cir. Sept. 24, 1999).

C. Public Distribution Right. 17 U.S.C. § 106(3).

1. The exclusive right to distribute to the public extends to every kind of copyrightable work.

2. The Copyright Act provides no definition of "distribution." The term, however, is viewed as essentially synonymous with "publication" and requires the dissemination of a material object. *See* Agee v. Paramount Communications, Inc., 59 F.3d 317 (2d Cir. 1995) (transmission of a work by satellite to television stations did not constitute a distribution). *Cf* Hotaling v. Church of Jesus Christ of Latter-Day Saints, 118 F.3d 199 (4th Cir. 1997) (listing work in library's catalog system, adding it to library's collection and making it available to the public constituted "distribution" of the work).

3. The copyright owner has the right to control the first public distribution of an authorized copy or phonorecord of the work, whether by sale, gift, loan or some rental or lease arrangement. *See* Burwood Co. v. Marsel Mirror & Glass Products, Inc., 468 F. Supp. 1215 (N.D. Ill. 1979).

4. Pursuant to the "first sale doctrine", the copyright owner's distribution right ceases with respect to a particular copy once the copyright owner has parted with ownership of that particular copy. 17 U.S.C. § 109(a). *See* Mirage Editions, Inc. v. Albuquerque A.R.T. Co., 856 F.2d 1341 (9th Cir. 1988), *cert. denied*, 489 U.S. 1018 (1989); C.M.

Paula Co. v. Logan, 355 F. Supp. 189 (N.D. Tex. 1973). Therefore, the owner of a lawfully made copy of the work may sell, rent or otherwise dispose of the possession of that copy.

a. The first sale doctrine no longer applies to the rental, lease or lending of a sound recording of a musical composition embodied in a phonorecord. 17 U.S.C. § 109(b)(1).

b. The first sale doctrine no longer applies to the rental, lease or lending of computer programs, except for those used in conjunction with a limited purpose computer that is designed for playing video games. 17 U.S.C. § 109(b)(1). *See* Central Point Software, Inc. v. Global Software & Accessories, Inc., 880 F. Supp. 957 (S.D.N.Y. 1995) (deferred billing program permitting purchasers to return a computer program after purchase for a service charge found to constitute rental, lease or lending prohibited by the statute).

c. The first sale doctrine applies to works originally manufactured in the United States for export, and then later imported into the United States. Quality King Distributors, Inc. v. L'anza Research International, Inc., 118 S. Ct. 1125 (1998).

d. The first sale doctrine has been limited for works that have had their copyrights restored by section 104A. 17 U.S.C. § 109(a).

(1) For non-reliance parties, copies or phonorecords of such restored works manufactured before January 1, 1996, may be sold or otherwise disposed of only for 12 months from that date.

(2) For reliance parties, the 12 month sell-off period begins on the earlier of the date of publication in the Federal Register of a notice of intent to enforce the restored copyright filed with the Copyright Office or the date of receipt by the reliance party of an actual notice of intent to enforce the restored copyright.

5. The owner of copyright in a collective work has the right to distribute to the public individual contributions as part of that particular collective work, any revision of that collective work, and any later collective work in the same series. 17 U.S.C. § 201(c). *See* Tasini v. New York Times Co., 1999 WL 753966, at *3-4 (2d Cir. Sept. 24, 1999).

6. One who distributes or offers to distribute copies or phonorecords containing the sounds or images of a live performance, made without the consent of the performer, is subject to the same remedies as an infringer of copyright. 17 U.S.C. § 1101.

D. Public Performance Right. 17 U.S.C. § 106(4).

1. The exclusive right to publicly perform a work extends to literary, musical, dramatic, and choreographic works, pantomimes, and motion pictures and other audiovisual works. The public performance need no longer be for profit.

a. To "perform" a work means to recite, render, play, dance or act it. 17 U.S.C. § 101 (definition of "perform").

(1) The playing of a game is not a "performance" within the meaning of the Copyright Act. Allen v. Academic Games League of America, Inc., 89 F.3d 614, 616 (Act should not be interpreted in a manner that would allow the owner of a copyright in a game to control when and where purchasers of games may play the games). *But see* Red Baron-Granklin Park, Inc. v. Taito Corp., 883 F.2d 275, 278-79 (4th Cir. 1989) (video game play in public arcade constituted public performance).

b. A "secondary transmission," the simultaneous retransmission of a primary transmission, is a performance. *See* Buck v. Jewell-La Salle Realty Co., 283 U.S. 191 (1931) (hotel's retransmission of a received radio signal into the hotel's lobby constituted an unauthorized performance).

2. The public nature of a performance is defined in § 101.

   a. Public place clause.

      (1) A performance is "public" if it occurs at a place open to the public or at any place where a substantial number of persons outside of a normal circle of a family and its social acquaintances is gathered. Sailor Music v. Gap Stores, Inc., 668 F.2d 84 (7th Cir. 1981), *cert. denied*, 456 U.S. 945 (1982); Columbia Pictures Industries, Inc. v. Redd Horne, Inc., 749 F.2d 154 (3d Cir. 1984).

      (2) Performances at "semipublic" places such as clubs, lodges and schools are now found to be public performances. 17 U.S.C. § 101.

      (3) Routine meetings of businesses and governmental personnel do not represent the gathering of a "substantial number of persons."

   b. Transmit clause.

      (1) A performance is "public" if it is transmitted to a place specified by the public place clause; or to a place or separate places where the public is capable of receiving the transmission at the same time or at different times.

      (2) The transmit clause applies only when images or sounds are transmitted from one place to another place. *See* Columbia Pictures Industries, Inc. v. Professional Real Estate Investors, Inc., 866 F.2d 278 (9th Cir. 1989) (transmit clause does not apply where video disk player in same room as television); *but see*, Columbia Pictures Industries, Inc. v. Aveco, Inc., 800 F.2d 59 (3d Cir. 1986).

      (3) The transmission of an image from a computer bulletin board, an on-line service or the Internet constitutes a public performance. *See* Playboy Enterprises v. Frena, 839 F. Supp. 1552 (M.D. Fla. 1993); On Command Video Corp. v. Columbia Pictures Indus., 777 F. Supp. 787 (N.D. Cal. 1991).

3. Small business exception.

   a. Reception of television and radio broadcasts on home-style receivers which may be seen or heard by the public is exempt so long as no direct charge is made. 17 U.S.C. § 110(5); *See* Twentieth Century Music Corp. v. Aiken, 422 U.S. 151 (1975).

   b. Courts use several factors in determining whether the exception applies. These factors include: the physical size of the business, the type of receiver used, whether the receiving apparatus was augmented, the number of speakers in the system, and whether the system was professionally installed. *See* Broadcast Music, Inc. v. Claire's Boutiques, Inc., 949 F.2d 1482 (7th Cir. 1991); Edison Brothers Stores, Inc. v. Broadcast Music, Inc., 954 F.2d 1419 (8th Cir. 1992). *But see* Springsteen v. Plaza Roller Dome, Inc., 602 F. Supp. 1113 (M.D.N.C. 1985) (defendant's insufficient financial ability to pay for a commercial background music service was held to place defendant within the exception).

   c. The unlicensed use of a music-on-hold device by a service station has been held to constitute an infringement outside of the small business exception. Prophet Music, Inc. v. Shamla Oil Co., Inc., 26 U.S.P.Q.2d 1554 (D. Minn. 1993).

   d. The reception by specified establishments of radio and television broadcasts or cable and satellite transmissions intended to be received by the general public may be exempted. 17 U.S.C. § 110(5)(B).

      (1) Non-food service or drinking establishments.

         (a) Establishments with less than 2,000 gross square feet of space (excluding space used for customer parking and for no other purpose); or

         (b) Establishments with 2,000 or more gross square feet of space, if

            i) the performance is audio only, the establishment has a total of not more than 6 loudspeakers, with no more than 4 loudspeakers located in any one room or adjoining outdoor space; or

ii) the performance or display is by audiovisual means, the establishment has a total of not more than 4 audiovisual devices (not greater than 55 inches), with no more than 1 audiovisual device in any 1 room, the audio portion is communicated by a total of not more than 6 loudspeakers, with no more than 4 loudspeakers located in any one room or adjoining outdoor space.

(2) Food service or drinking establishments.

(a) Establishments with less than 3,750 gross square feet of space (excluding space used for customer parking and for no other purpose); or

(b) Establishments with 3,750 or more gross square feet of space, if

i) the performance is audio only, the establishment has a total of not more than 6 loudspeakers, with no more than 4 loudspeakers located in any one room or adjoining outdoor space; or

ii) the performance or display is by audiovisual means, the establishment has a total of not more than 4 audiovisual devices (not greater than 55 inches), with no more than 1 audiovisual device in any 1 room, the audio portion is communicated by a total of not more than 6 loudspeakers, with no more than 4 loudspeakers located in any one room or adjoining outdoor space.

e. Determination of license fees.

(1) Proprietor who owns or operates fewer than 7 non-publicly traded establishments may challenge the reasonableness of license fees sought by

ASCAP or BMI and request a judicial determination of a reasonable license fee in either the Southern District of New York or the circuit in which the proprietor's business is located. 17 U.S.C. § 512.

f. Enhanced damages.

(1) In any case in which the defendant did not have reasonable grounds for asserting § 110(5) as a defense, the plaintiff shall be entitled to an award of two times the amount of the license fee that the defendant should have paid (up to 3 years), in addition to any award of damages. 17 U.S.C. § 504(d).

4. Certain face to face teaching activities are exempted from the public performance provision. 17 U.S.C. § 110(1).

5. Certain nonprofit performances are exempted from the public performance provision. 17 U.S.C. § 110(4).

6. Vendor Exemption.

a. A vending establishment that performs nondramatic musical works to promote the retail sale of copies or phonorecords of the work, or to promote audiovisual or other devices, is exempted from the public performance provision. 17 U.S.C. § 110(7).

7. Except for a limited digital transmission right provided by § 106(6), there is no public performance right for sound recordings. 17 U.S.C. § 114.

8. Unauthorized recording of live musical performances.

a. The Uruguay Round Agreements Act, implementing the General Agreement on Tariffs and Trade ("GATT"), has made one who "transmits or otherwise communicates to the public the sounds or sounds and images of a live musical performance," without the consent of the performer, subject to the same remedies as an infringer of copyright. 17 U.S.C. § 1101.

E. Public Display Right. 17 U.S.C. § 106(5).

1. The exclusive right to publicly display a work extends to literary, musical, dramatic, and choreographic works, pantomimes, and pictorial, graphic, or sculptural works, including the individual images of a motion picture or other audiovisual work. *See* Burwood Co. v. Marsel Mirror & Glass Products, Inc., 468 F. Supp. 1215 (N.D. Ill 1979).

2. The owner of a lawfully made copy of a work is entitled, without the authority of the copyright owner, to display that copy publicly. 17 U.S.C. § 109(c).

F. Digital Public Performance Right For Sound Recordings. 17 U.S.C. § 106(6).

1. The Digital Performance Right in Sound Recordings Act of 1995 provides protected sound recordings with a limited public performance right by means of digital audio transmission.

   a. Copyright owners of sound recordings have a limited exclusive right to publicly perform their works by means of digital audio transmissions. 17 U.S.C. § 106(6).

   b. Limitations have been placed on consensual licenses for interactive transmissions.

      (1) A "most favored nations" provision may be applied to transmission licenses. 17 U.S.C. § 114(h).

      (2) Time limitations may be placed on exclusive interactive licenses. 17 U.S.C. § 114(d)(3).

   c. Various public performances of sound recordings have been exempted, including nonsubscription transmissions (such as radio broadcasts) and retransmissions of radio broadcasts. 17 U.S.C. § 114(d)(1).

2. Public performances of sound recordings by a noninteractive digital transmission may qualify for a "statutory license" (compulsory license). 17 U.S.C. § 114(d)(2).

   a. To qualify for the "statutory license," the transmission must meet 12 conditions, including a limitation on the number of recordings from a single album or artist transmitted during a specified time period and a prohibition of advance announcements of playlists.

b. The "statutory license" rate will be determined by a Copyright Arbitration Royalty Panel, unless a voluntary industry agreement is reached.

(1) The statutory licensing fees will be disbursed as follows, 17 U.S.C. § 114(g)(2):

(a) 50% to record companies.

(b) 45% to featured performers.

(c) 2 1/2% to AFM musicians.

(d) 2 1/2% to AFTRA performers.

3. Public performances of sound recordings by an interactive digital transmission, or a noninteractive digital transmission that does not qualify for a "statutory license" requires a negotiated license from the owner of the copyright in the sound recording.

G. Moral Rights Are Generally Not Protected by United States Copyright law.

1. United States copyright law seeks to vindicate the economic, rather than the personal, rights of authors, therefore moral rights are generally not recognized as a part of copyright law. *See* Crimi v. Rutgers Presbyterian Church, 194 Misc. 570, 89 N.Y.S.2d 813 (Sup. Ct. 1949); Gilliam v. American Broadcasting Companies, Inc., 538 F.2d 14 (2d Cir. 1976).

2. As a general rule, United States copyright law does not recognize a right of attribution. *See* Graham v. James, 144 F.3d 229, 236 (2d Cir. 1998) (author who sells or licenses her work does not have an inherent right to be credited as its author).

3. Moral rights have been specifically accorded only to a limited category of works of visual art pursuant to the Visual Artists Rights Act of 1990 ("VARA"). 17 U.S.C. § 106A. *See* Carter v. Helmsley-Spear, Inc., 71 F.3d 77 (2d Cir. 1995), *cert. denied*, 517 U.S. 1208 (1996).

a. Section 106A protects the moral rights of the author, not the economic rights of the copyright owner.

b. "Work of visual art" defined (17 U.S.C. § 101).

(1) The initial rendering of a painting, drawing, print or sculpture and any copy in a limited edition of 200 copies or fewer if the copies are signed and consecutively numbered by the author.

(2) The initial rendering of a still photographic image which was produced for exhibition purposes only and signed by the author. Any copy in a limited edition of 200 copies or fewer is also protected if the copies are signed and consecutively numbered by the author.

(3) The moral rights of § 106A do not apply to commercial uses of work, nor to a work made for hire. 17 U.S.C. § 106A(c).

c. Protection granted by VARA.

(1) Attribution.

(a) An author has the right to claim authorship in her work, to prevent the use of her name as the author of any work she did not create and to prevent the use of her name as the author of a work she did originally create, but which has been mutilated. 17 U.S.C. § 106A(a)(1-2).

(2) Integrity.

(a) An author has the right to prevent the intentional distortion, mutilation, or other modification of her work that would be prejudicial to her honor or reputation. 17 U.S.C. § 106A(a)(3)(A).

(b) An author has the right to prevent any intentional or grossly negligent destruction of her work. 17 U.S.C. § 106A(a)(3)(B).

d. The moral rights in a work of visual art that has been incorporated in or made part of a building may be protected. 17 U.S.C. § 113(d).

   (1) Removal of a work of visual art.

      (a) If work cannot be removed without its destruction, distortion, mutilation, or other modification, the author's attribution and integrity rights will be protected unless:

         i) The author consented to the installation of the work in the building before June 1, 1991, 17 U.S.C. § 113(d)(1)(B), or

         ii) On or after June 1, 1991, the author consented to the installation of the work in the building in a written instrument, signed by the owner of the building and the author, that specifies that installation of the work may subject it to destruction, distortion, mutilation, or other modification by reason of its removal. 17 U.S.C. § 113(d)(1)(B).

      (b) If work can be removed without its destruction, distortion, mutilation, or other modification, the author's attribution and integrity rights will be protected unless:

         i) The owner of the building has made a diligent, good faith attempt without success to notify the author of the intended removal, 17 U.S.C. § 113(d)(2)(A), or

         ii) The owner of the building provided written notice, but the person so notified failed either to remove the work or to pay for its removal within 90 days after receiving the notice. 17 U.S.C. § 113(d)(2)(B).

      (c) If the work is removed at the expense of the author, title to the removed copy of the work is deemed to be in the author. 17 U.S.C. § 113(d)(2).

e. The moral rights of an author protected by § 106A may not be transferred, but they may be waived in a written instrument signed by the author. 17 U.S.C. § 106A(e).

f. Duration of VARA rights.

(1) For works of visual art created on or after June 1, 1991, the duration of rights under § 106A is life of the author. 17 U.S.C. § 106A(d)(1).

(2) For works of visual art created prior to June 1, 1991, the title to which was not transferred from the author as of June 1, 1991, the duration of rights under § 106A is life of the author plus 70 years. 17 U.S.C. § 106A(d)(2).

g. All civil remedies for copyright infringement granted under the Copyright Act are available to plaintiffs who bring suit under VARA. Martin v. City of Indianapolis, 4 F. Supp. 2d 808, 809 (S.D. Ind. 1998).

4. The exclusive right to make or authorize the making of a derivative work has been interpreted as protecting, to some degree, the moral rights of authors. *See* Gilliam v. American Broadcasting Companies, Inc., 538 F.2d 14 (2d Cir. 1976).

5. Moral rights may be protected under legal theories other than copyright law. *See e.g.* Gilliam v. American Broadcasting Companies, Inc., 538 F.2d 14 (2d Cir. 1976) (§ 43(a) of the Lanham Act); Preminger v. Columbia Pictures Corp., 267 N.Y.S.2d 594 (Sup. Ct. 1966), *aff'd*, 25 A.D.2d 830, 269 N.Y.S.2d 913 (1966), aff'd, 150 U.S.P.Q. 829 (N.Y. Ct. App. 1966) (unfair competition); Granz v. Harris, 198 F.2d 585 (2d Cir. 1952) (breach of contract); Clevenger v. Baker, Voorhis & Co., 8 N.Y.2d 187, 168 N.E.2d 643 (1960) (defamation).

6. State legislation has been passed to provide protection of the moral rights of authors. *See e.g.* Cal. Civ. Code §§ 987, 989; Mass. Gen Laws Ann. ch. 231, § 85S; N.Y. Arts & Cultural Affairs Law §§ 14.51-14.59. *See* Wojnarowicz v. American Family Association, 745 F. Supp. 130 (S.D.N.Y. 1990); Botello v. Shell Oil Co., 229 Cal. App. 3d 1130, 280 Cal. Rptr. 535 (1991). The recently created federal moral

rights protection may constrain these state statutes or preempt them entirely. *See* 17 U.S.C. § 301(f).

VI. FORMALITIES OF PROTECTION.

A. Publication and Notice Requirement.

1. The date of publication determines the need for a copyright notice. Different rules apply depending on whether the work was published under the 1909 Act (1909-1977), during the decennial period (1-1-78 to 2-28-89), or on or after March 1, 1989.

2. 1909 Act (1909-1977).

a. A proper copyright notice was required on any work which underwent a general publication.

(1) A general publication occurs when a possessory interest in tangible copies of the work is made available to the general public. Burke v. National Broadcasting Co., 598 F.2d 688 (1st Cir.), *cert. denied*, 444 U.S. 869 (1979); Data Cash Sys., Inc. v. JS&A Group, Inc., 628 F.2d 1039 (7th Cir. 1980). *Cf.* Dolman v. Agee, 157 F.3d 708, 714 (9th Cir. 1998) (copyright certificates listing publication dates of Laurel & Hardy movies insufficient evidence to prove divesting publication).

(2) In response to a split between the Ninth and Second Circuits as to whether the distribution of phonorecords containing a musical composition to the public is a general publication that requires the use of a proper copyright notice to protect the copyright in the musical composition, *see* La Cienega Music Co. v. ZZ Top, 3 F.3d 950 (9th Cir. 1995) (general publication); Rosette v. Rainbo Record Mfg. Corp., 354 F. Supp. 1183 (S.D.N.Y. 1973), *aff'd per curiam*, 546 F.2d 461 (2d Cir. 1976) (phonorecord held not to be a copy of musical composition), Congress decided that any distribution of a phonorecord before January 1, 1978, did not

constitute a publication of a musical composition embodied within it. 17 U.S.C. § 303(b).

(3) An unpublished screenplay protected by common law is published by a motion picture to the extent the screenplay is incorporated into the film. *See* Batjac Productions Inc. v. Goodtimes Home Video Corp., 160 F.3d 1223, 1233 (9th Cir. 1998); Classic Film Museum, Inc. v. Warner Bros., Inc., 453 F. Supp. 852 (D. Me. 1978), *aff'd*, 597 F.2d 13 (1st Cir. 1979).

(4) Because United States copyright law has no extraterritorial effect, publication of a foreign work outside the United States without copyright notice did not place the work in the public domain. *See* Twin Books Corp. v. Walt Disney Co., 83 F.3d 1162, 1167 (9th Cir. 1996); Heim v. Universal Pictures Co., Inc., 154 F.2d 480 (2d Cir. 1946).

(5) A performance does not constitute a publication. *See* Estate of Martin Luther King, Jr., Inc. v. CBS, Inc., 194 F.3d 1211, 1215-16 (2d Cir. 1999); American Vitagraph, Inc. v. Levy, 659 F.2d 1023, 1027 (9th Cir. 1981); Burke v. National Broadcasting Co., 598 F.2d 688 (1st Cir.), *cert. denied*, 444 U.S. 869 (1979).

b. No copyright notice is required when the distribution of the work constitutes a "limited publication." A limited publication occurs when tangible copies of the work are distributed to a limited class of persons and for a limited purpose. Academy of Motion Picture Arts and Sciences v. Creative House Promotions, Inc., 944 F.2d 1446 (9th Cir. 1991) ("Oscar" statuette underwent only limited publication and is not in the public domain); White v. Kimmell, 193 F.2d 744, 746-47 (9th Cir. 1952).

c. The copyright notice requirement was excused where the notice was omitted from no more than a relatively small number of copies.

d. Copyright notice was required when a work was publicly displayed. *See* American Tobacco Co. v. Werckmeister, 207 U.S. 284 (1907).

(1) The notice requirement was excused where copying of the publicly displayed work was prohibited and the restriction was enforced by guards. *See* Letter Edged in Black Press, Inc. v. Public Bldg. Comm'n of Chicago, 320 F. Supp. 1303, 1311 (N.D. Ill. 1970).

e. Failure to meet the notice requirement led to harsh results. General publication of a work without proper copyright notice immediately and irreversibly divested the work of copyright protection, placing it into the public domain. *See* Letter Edged in Black Press, Inc. v. Public Bldg. Comm'n of Chicago, 320 F. Supp. 1303 (N.D. Ill. 1970); J.A. Richards, Inc. v. New York Post, Inc., 23 F. Supp. 619 (S.D.N.Y. 1938).

3. Decennial period (1-1-78 through 2-28-89).

a. A proper notice of copyright was required on all publicly distributed copies of a work which had undergone a general publication in the United States or elsewhere by authority of the copyright owner. 17 U.S.C. § 401(a).

(1) The definitions of general publication and limited publication remained unchanged from the 1909 Act.

b. The 1976 Copyright Act treated the omission of copyright notice less harshly than the 1909 Act. The omission of proper copyright notice could be cured under certain circumstances, saving the work from the public domain. 17 U.S.C. § 405. *See* Hasbro Bradley, Inc. v. Sparkle Toys, Inc., 780 F.2d 189 (2d Cir. 1985); Florists' Transworld Delivery Association v. Reliable Glassware & Pottery Co., Inc., 213 U.S.P.Q. 808 (N.D. Ill. 1981); Original Appalachian Artworks, Inc. v. Toy Loft, Inc., 684 F.2d 821 (11th Cir. 1982). The omission was excused and the copyright in the work was not invalidated if:

(1) The notice had been omitted from no more than a relatively small number of copies or phonorecords distributed to the general public; or

(a) Notice omitted from 1,500 works is more than a relatively small number of copies. Foamation, Inc. v. Wedeward Enterprises, Inc., 970 F. Supp. 676 (E.D. Wis. 1997).

(2) Where the notice has been omitted from more than a small number of copies or phonorecords:

(a) Registration of the work with the U.S. Copyright Office has been made before or is made within five years after the publication without notice; and

(b) A reasonable effort, within a reasonable period of time, is made to add notice to all copies or phonorecords that were distributed to the public in the United States after the omission was discovered; or

(3) The notice was omitted in violation of a written agreement that the copies or phonorecords distributed to the general public bear the prescribed notice.

c. Liability of an innocent infringer who relied upon the omission of copyright notice does not include actual or statutory damages. In addition to recovery of the infringer's profits and an injunction, a court is empowered to require the payment of a reasonable license fee. 17 U.S.C. § 405(b).

d. An innocent infringer who obtained, in good faith, a transfer or license from a person improperly named in the copyright notice has a complete defense to a copyright infringement action brought by copyright owner. The person improperly named in the copyright notice is liable for all receipts from transfers or licenses purportedly made under the copyright. 17 U.S.C. § 406(a). *See* Bagdadi v. Nazar, 84 F.3d 1194 (9th Cir. 1996).

(1) The innocent infringer will not be found to have acted in good faith if the work had been registered in the name of the copyright owner or a document showing the ownership of copyright had been recorded.

4. On or after March 1, 1989.

   a. Copyright notice is no longer required on any published work. It is strongly suggested, however, that copyright owners continue to use copyright notice.

   b. Use of copyright notice precludes the ability of a defendant to mitigate damages pursuant to an innocent infringement defense. 17 U.S.C. §§ 401(d), 402(d).

   c. The failure to place a proper copyright notice on publicly distributed works prior to March 1, 1989, continues to be relevant as such failure may have placed the work in the public domain. As a result, there is no copyright in the work to enforce. *See, e.g.*, Charles Garnier, Paris v. Andin Int'l, Inc., 36 F.3d 1214 (1st Cir. 1994); La Cienega Music Co. v. ZZ Top, 3 F.3d 950 (9th Cir. 1995).

B. Form of Notice.

1. The copyright notice form consists or three elements:

   a. The symbol © (the letter C in a circle), or the word "Copyright", or the abbreviation "Copr."; or the symbol ℗ (the letter P in a circle) when the work is a sound recording; and

   b. The year of first publication of the work; and

      (1) In the case of compilations or derivative works incorporating previously published material, the year date of first publication of the compilation or derivative work is sufficient.

      (2) The year date may be omitted where a pictorial, graphic, or sculptural work is reproduced in or on greeting cards, postcards, stationary, jewelry, dolls, toys, or any useful articles.

c. The name of the owner of the copyright in the work.

(1) An abbreviation by which the name of the owner of copyright can be recognized, or a generally known alternative designation of the owner may be used.

2. Collective work blanket notice provision.

a. The copyright notice regarding the copyright in a collective work, such as a magazine, is sufficient to satisfy the copyright notice requirements with respect to the separate contributions it contains. 17 U.S.C. § 404(a).

b. This blanket notice provision does not apply to advertisements placed in the collective work. Such advertisements require an independent copyright notice. 17 U.S.C. § 404(a).

c. There is a presumption that a copyright notice in a collective work pertains only to the collective work and not the individual works which comprise the collective work. 17 U.S.C. § 201(c).

C. Registration and Deposit.

1. Registration and deposit are not required to acquire a federal copyright in a work. Such protection automatically exists at the time of creation/fixation. *See* Kodadek v. MTV Networks, Inc., 152 F.3d 1209, 1211 (9th Cir. 1998).

2. The Copyright Act has a mandatory deposit provision which requires the copyright owner to deposit two copies of a published work with the Library of Congress. 17 U.S.C. § 407.

3. Registration as a prerequisite to filing a copyright infringement action.

a. Registration is not a prerequisite to filing a copyright infringement action where the work at issue is a "Berne Convention work" whose country of origin is not the United States. 17 U.S.C. § 411.

b. Where the work was first published in the United States, or where the author is a U.S. national, the copyright in the work must be registered prior to instituting a copyright infringement action.

(1) The date of registration is the date on which the Copyright Office has received the application, deposit and payment.

(2) An unsuccessful applicant may file an action for copyright infringement so long as the Copyright Office is notified.

4. Registration procedures.

a. Submission of an application on the appropriate official form.

(1) Fill-in copyright registration forms are available on the Copyright Office Website at www.loc.gov/copyright.

b. Deposit of a single copy for unpublished works or two copies for published works. This deposit satisfies the mandatory deposit provision of § 407.

c. A registration fee of $30.00.

5. When the registration is completed, the copyright owner receives a certificate of registration. This certificate constitutes prima facie evidence of the validity of the copyright and of the facts stated in the certificate if registration was made before or within five years after the first publication of the work. 17 U.S.C. § 410(c); Evans and Assocs. Inc. v. Continental Homes, Inc., 785 F.2d 897, 903 (11th Cir. 1986).

VII. LENGTH OF PROTECTION.

A. Duration of works subject to the 1976 Copyright Act.

1. Works created on or after January 1, 1978.

a. Works by an individual author. 17 U.S.C. § 302(a).

(1) The term of copyright protection consists of the life of the author plus 70 years after his/her death.

b. Joint works. 17 U.S.C. § 302(b).

(1) The term of copyright protection is the life of the last surviving co-author plus 70 years after his/her death.

c. Anonymous works (no author identified); Pseudonymous works (fictitious name); and Works made for hire. 17 U.S.C. § 302(c).

(1) The term of copyright protection is 95 years after the work's first publication or 120 years after its creation, whichever is earlier.

2. Works created but not published or registered before January 1, 1978. 17 U.S.C. § 303.

a. These works were protected by state common law copyright when the 1976 Copyright Act took effect on January 1, 1978. They have now lost their perpetual common law protection and receive the same duration of protection as those works created on or after January 1, 1978.

b. In no case, however, will the protection of these works expire prior to December 31, 2002. If the work is published between January 1, 1978 and December 31, 2002, copyright protection will not expire before December 31, 2047.

3. Works already protected by federal copyright law when the 1976 Copyright Act took effect on January 1, 1978.

a. Under the 1909 Copyright Act, federal statutory protection was given for 28 years from the date the work was invested with federal protection. A work was invested with federal protection when it was published with proper copyright notice or when it was registered with the Copyright Office. Federal protection could be extended for a second term of 28 years if the copyright was renewed by the copyright owner. If the copyright in the work was not renewed, it entered the public domain at the end of the 28th year. Under the 1909 Copyright Act, all works had the same duration of copyright.

b. Interim Renewal Term Extension.

(1) Any renewal terms of federal copyright protection which would have expired between September 19, 1962, and December 31, 1977, were automatically continued through December 31, 1977 and brought into the new Act. These interim extensions of copyright protection were periodically passed by Congress in anticipation of the "new" Copyright Act extending the renewal terms still further. As of January 1, 1978, these works, which were previously protected by the 1909 Copyright Act, obtained the protection of the 1976 Act. Specific duration rules are then applied which provide copyright protection for 75 years from the date federal protection initially vested, unless the renewal occurred after 1950, in which case copyright protection is provided for 95 years from the date federal protection initially vested. 17 U.S.C. § 304.

c. Statutorily protected works which were in their initial term (first 28 years) of protection on January 1, 1978. 17 U.S.C. § 304(a).

(1) The copyright in the work may be renewed by the author during the 28th year of the initial period of copyright protection. If the author is deceased, the author's statutory heirs may renew the copyright. The statutory heirs are the spouse and any children. If none are alive, then the author's executor. If the author left no will, then the author's next of kin. 17 U.S.C. § 304(a)(1)(C); Jeffrey M. Lowy, *When Does the Renewal Term Vest: Before and After the Copyright Renewal Act of 1992*, 13 Loy. L.A. Ent. L.J. 437 (1993).

(2) The renewal period has been extended from 28 to 67 years. The total term of federal copyright protection is 95 years.

(a) The 28 year renewal term of the 1909 Act was extended to 47 years in 1978, and further extended to 67 years in 1998.

(3) In 1992, the Copyright Act was amended to make renewal automatic. The automatic renewal applies to any work which was initially invested with federal protection from 1964 through 1977.

(a) Advantages of filing a renewal: Even though renewal is now automatic, it is advantageous to file a renewal with the Copyright Office.

i) The renewal certificate constitutes prima facie evidence of copyright validity.

ii) The renewal certificate constitutes prima facie evidence of copyright ownership.

iii) The filing of a renewal in the 28th year permits the copyright owner to take advantage of the U.S. Supreme Court decision in Stewart v. Abend, 495 U.S. 207 (1990).

a) The Abend decision held that the creator of a derivative work could not continue to utilize its derivative work after the copyright in the underlying work was renewed by statutory heirs, unless it was licensed by the statutory heirs. *See* Eric Early, *Its a Wonderful Life - Motion Picture Studios Can Regain Control of Their Wayward Classics*, 1 UCLA Ent. L.J. 139 (1994).

b) The Abend "problem" may arise only when all of the following conditions occur: (1) The copyright must be assigned or licensed prior to its renewal; (2) The author must die prior to renewal; and (3) The statutory heirs must file a renewal with the Copyright Office in the 28th year of the initial term of protection.

c) The failure to file a renewal in the 28th year will excuse the creator of a derivative work from the Abend decision and grant a "continued use" exception to the owner of the derivative work that can be used as a defense to a copyright infringement action brought by the statutory heirs.

d. Statutorily protected works which are in their renewal term of protection on January 1, 1978. 17 U.S.C. § 304(b).

(1) Protection of these works was automatically extended to a total of 75 years from the date federal statutory protection was first secured.

(a) The 28 year renewal term under the 1909 Act was increased to 47 years.

(2) Any work still in its renewal term in 1998 is protected for a total of 95 years from the date federal statutory protection was first secured.

(a) The 47 year renewal term under the 1976 Act was increased to 67 years.

(b) Any copyright that went into the public domain prior to 1998 will not be resurrected and will not receive an additional 20 years of protection.

(3) No additional renewal with the Copyright Office is required.

B. Statutory Termination of Grants.

1. Post-1977 Transfers and Licenses Granted by the Author.

Under the 1976 Act, reversion of rights back to the author occurs through termination of transfers and nonexclusive licenses rather than the approach under the 1909 Act that allowed a reversion at the end of the 28 year initial term of copyright protection. 17 U.S.C. § 203.

a. Types of grants to which the termination provisions apply.

(1) Any "transfer" of copyright executed by the author on or after January 1, 1978.

(a) A "transfer" includes the assignment, exclusive license or conveyance of a copyright or of any of the exclusive rights comprised in a copyright. 17 U.S.C. § 101.

(b) A mortgage is considered a transfer of copyright ownership and is subject to termination.

(2) Nonexclusive licenses executed by the author on or after January 1, 1978.

b. Types of grants not subject to termination.

(1) Grants by will.

(2) Transfers not executed by the author. E.g., by successors in interest.

(3) Works made for hire.

c. Rights subject to termination.

(1) Only those rights which were the subject of the original grant will revert upon the termination of that grant.

(2) Foreign rights are not affected by termination. A grant of copyright "throughout the world" is terminable only with respect to uses within the geographic limits of the United States. Copyright laws do not have extraterritorial operation.

(3) Statutory exclusion for derivative works.

(a) "A derivative work prepared under authority of the grant before its termination may continue to be utilized under the terms of the grant after its termination, but this privilege does not extend to the preparation after the termination of other derivative works based upon the copyrighted work covered by the terminated grant." 17 U.S.C. § 203(b)(1).

(b) The House Report states that for the purpose of construing this continuing right to utilize a derivative work after termination, a motion picture would be considered a "derivative work" with respect to every "preexisting work" incorporated in it, whether the preexisting work was created independently (as in the case of a novel) or was prepared expressly for the motion picture (as in the case of a screenplay which might otherwise be viewed as a joint work). [H. Rep. at 127]

d. Persons who may terminate.

(1) Author.

Termination may be affected by the author, if alive at the time when termination can be made. The estate of the author may terminate the grant only if the author died after the notice of termination has been served.

(2) Joint authors.

(a) In the case of a grant executed by two or more authors of a joint work, termination of the grant must be effected by a "majority of the authors who executed" the grant.

(b) If any of the joint authors is dead, the termination interest of such deceased joint author may be exercised by the person or persons who own and are entitled to exercise a total of more than one-half of that joint author's interest.

(3) Statutory successors.

Where the author is dead, his or her termination interest is owned and may be exercised by the widow, widower, children, grandchildren, executor, administrator, personal representative or trustee as set forth in § 203(a)(2).

e. Mechanics of termination.

(1) When grants may be terminated.

(a) The author or the author's statutory successor is permitted to terminate the grant of rights 35 years after the initial grant. The grant may be terminated any time during the five year period beginning at the end of the 35 years from the date of execution of the grant. § 203(a)(3). The author or statutory successor must actually terminate the grant of rights pursuant to the requirements stated in the statute. If termination is made, all of the rights granted away revert to the author or the author's statutory successor.

i) An exception has been made for grants which include the right of publication. Where the "right of publication" has been granted, the termination window begins at the end of the 40th year from the date of the grant, unless the work is published within five years of the grant, in which case the termination window begins at the end of the 35th year from the date of publication.

(b) Licenses of indefinite duration.

i) A split of authority exists as to whether section 203 imposes a 35-year term for a license of indefinite duration that would otherwise be subject to earlier termination under state contract law. *Compare* Korman v. HBC Florida, Inc., 182 F.3d 1291 (11th Cir. 1999), *and* Walthal v. Rusk, 172 F.3d 481 (7th Cir. 1999) (section 203 does not create a minimum term of 35 years for licenses of indefinite duration and thus does not preempt state law), *with* Rano v. Sipa Press, Inc., 987 F.2d 580, 585 (9th Cir. 1993) (license of indefinite duration terminable at will of the author only during a five year period beginning at the end of the thirty-five years from the date of the execution of the license, contrary state law is preempted).

(2) Termination notice.

(a) Must be served on grantee or grantee's successor in title.

(b) Notice must state the effective date of termination.

(c) Notice must be served not less than two nor more than ten years before the date of termination specified in the notice. See time line set forth below.

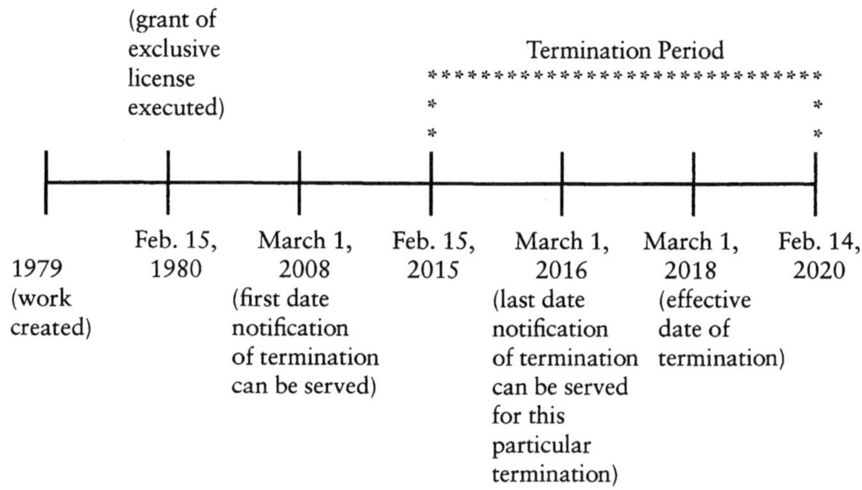

(d) Notice must be in writing.

(e) Owner of termination interest or an authorized agent must sign the notice.

(f) Notice must be recorded in the United States Copyright Office prior to date of termination.

(g) Form, content and manner of service can be found in the Copyright Office regulations.

f. Further grants of reverted rights.

Further grants after termination may be made by the same number and proportion of the owners as were required to terminate the grant. 17 U.S.C. § 203(b)(3).

g. Failure to terminate.

(1) An unlimited grant of rights that is not terminated will continue in effect for the duration of the term of copyright. 17 U.S.C. § 203(b)(6).

(2) Failure to terminate does not extend the duration of any license, transfer, or assignment made for a period of less than 35 years. Where a transfer or license agreement provides for an earlier termination date or a shorter duration, or where it permits the author the right to cancel or terminate the agreement under certain conditions, the contractual provisions govern. Korman v. HBC Florida, Inc., 182 F.3d 1291, 1295 (11th Cir. 1999).

h. Termination right may not be assigned away.

(1) An agreement not to terminate is not valid. 17 U.S.C. § 203(a)(5).

(2) An agreement to make a grant after termination is valid only if it is made after the effective date of termination. 17 U.S.C. § 203(b)(4).

(a) An agreement with the original grantee or its successor in title to make a grant after termination is valid if made after the notice of termination is given, but before the date of termination. 17 U.S.C. § 203(b)(4).

2. Pre-1978 Transfers and Licenses Granted by the Author.

a. The duration of all copyrights renewed before January 1, 1978, and in their second term of protection as of that date, were extended automatically for an additional period of 19 years. In 1998, an additional 20 years were added to the renewal term. Section 304(c) provides for the termination and recapture of this extended 39 year term.

b. First term statutory copyrights in existence on January 1, 1978, which were affirmatively renewed between 1978 and 1991, or were automatically renewed after 1991, are renewed for a second term of 67 years (an additional 39 years added to the 28 year renewal term available under the 1909 Act). Section 304(c) also provides for the termination of this extended 39-year period.

c. The author or the author's statutory beneficiary is permitted to take advantage of the 39 years of protection which were added to the renewal period by the 1976 Copyright Act. The author or statutory beneficiary must actually terminate the grant of rights pursuant to the requirements stated in the statute. If termination is made, all of the rights granted away revert to the author or the author's statutory beneficiary. If no termination is made, the grantee takes advantage of the additional 39 years. *See* Burroughs v. Metro-Goldwyn-Mayer, Inc., 683 F.2d 610 (2d Cir. 1982).

d. Types of grants subject to termination.

    (1) Any grant of rights covering the renewal copyright in the work, executed by the author or those beneficiaries of the author who can claim renewal, before January 1, 1978, may be terminated.

e. Types of grants not subject to termination.

    (1) Grants made by will.

    (2) Grants of works made for hire.

f. Rights subject to termination.

    (1) Only those rights which were the subject of the original grant will revert upon the termination of that grant.

    (2) Foreign rights are not affected by termination.

    (3) Statutory exclusion for derivative work.

        (a) "A derivative work prepared under authority of the grant before its termination may continue to be utilized under the terms of the grant after its termination, but this privilege does not extend to the preparation after the termination of other derivative works based upon the copyrighted work covered by the terminated grant." § 304(c)(6)(A).

(b) Granting of a synchronization license for use of a pre-termination sound recording in a post-termination motion picture and a mechanical license for its soundtrack album fell outside the derivative work exception. Fred Ahlert Music Corp. v. Warner/Chappell Music, inc., 155 F.3d 17 (2d Cir. 1998) (mechanical license for pre-termination sound recording limited to use in a specific album).

(c) A music publisher may continue to receive its share of royalties derived from the sale of pre-termination licensed recordings of a musical composition after the termination of the grant to the music publisher of the copyright in the musical composition. Mills Music, Inc. v. Snyder, 469 U.S. 153 (1985).

(d) A music publisher may continue to receive royalties from public performances of a musical arrangement contained in a pre-termination audiovisual work after the termination of the grant to the music publisher of the copyright in the musical composition. Woods v. Bourne Co., 60 F.3d 978 (2d Cir. 1995).

g. Persons who may terminate.

(1) Author.

(2) Statutory successors.

(a) If the grant was made by an individual author, she or a majority of her surviving spouse and children, or grandchildren, may effect termination. In the event that the spouse, children and grandchildren are deceased, the author's executor, administrator, personal representative or trustee may effect termination. 17 U.S.C. § 304(c)(2).

(b) If the grant was made by joint authors, each author may terminate separately as to her interest in the work.

(c) If the grant was executed by a person or persons other than the author, termination can only be effected by the "unanimous action" of the surviving person or persons who executed it.

h. Mechanics of termination.

(1) When grants may be terminated.

(a) Termination of pre-1978 grants may be effected at any time during the five year period beginning at the end of 56 years from the date statutory copyright was originally secured, or beginning on January 1, 1978, whichever is later. See time line set forth below.

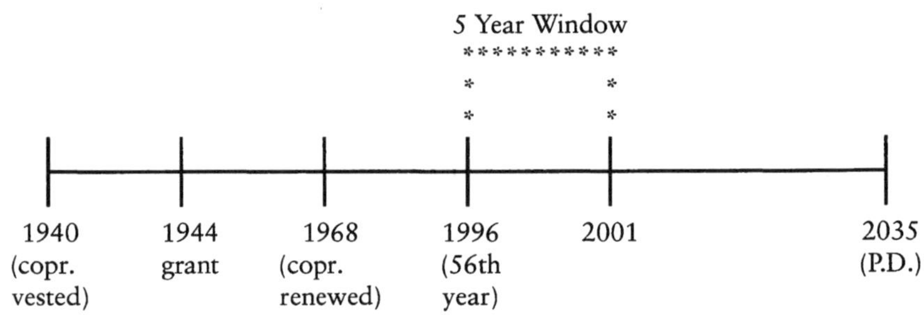

(b) If the work's renewal period was affected by the interim extensions (Sept. 19, 1962—Dec. 31, 1977), the five year period begins on January 1, 1978, if later in time.

(c) If the five year termination right arising at the end of the 56th year of federal copyright protection had expired by October 27, 1998, without being exercised, the grant may be terminated at any time during the five year period beginning at the end of 75 years from the date statutory copyright was originally secured. 17 U.S.C. § 304(d).

(2) Termination notice.

(a) Must be served on grantee or grantee's successor in title.

(b) Notice must state the effective date of termination.

(c) Notice must be served not less than two nor more than ten years before the date of termination specified in the notice.

(d) Notice must be in writing.

(e) Owner of termination interest or an authorized agent must sign the notice.

i) If an author-executed grant is being terminated the notice must be signed by the author or authors, a duly authorized agent thereof, or, if such author is dead, by a majority of those who own the deceased author's termination interest.

a) A non-executing joint author may not terminate nor may such author's successors.

ii) If the grant was executed by persons other than the author (non-author executed grant), the notice must be signed by all persons who are entitled to terminate.

(f) Notice must be recorded in the United States Copyright Office prior to date of termination.

(g) Form, content and manner of service can be found in the Copyright Office regulations.

i Failure to terminate.

(1) An unlimited grant of rights that is not terminated will continue in effect for the duration of the term of copyright.

(2) Failure to terminate does not extend the duration of any license, transfer, or assignment made for a period of less than 56 years. Where a transfer or license agreement provides for an earlier termination date or a shorter duration, or where it permits the author the right to cancel or terminate the agreement under certain conditions, the contractual provisions govern.

j. Termination right may not be assigned away.

(1) An agreement not to terminate is not valid. 17 U.S.C. § 304(c)(5).

(2) An agreement to make a grant after termination is valid only if it is made after the effective date of termination. 17 U.S.C. § 304(c)(6)(D).

(a) An agreement with the original grantee or its successor in title to make a grant after termination is valid if made after the notice of termination is given, but before the date of termination. 17 U.S.C. § 304(c)(6)(D).

k. Second statutory termination opportunity.

In 1998, Congress created a second termination opportunity for grants that had not been terminated after the 56th year of copyright protection, but now benefit from a 20 year extension of the renewal term.

(1) The pre-1978 grant of a copyright transfer or license may be terminated within a five year termination window that begins at the end of 75 years from the date statutory copyright was originally secured, if:

(a) The five year termination right arising at the end of the 56th year of federal copyright protection had expired by October 27, 1998, and

(b) The five year termination right arising at the end of the 56th year of federal copyright protection had not been exercised. 17 U.S.C. § 304(d).

(2) This additional termination opportunity does not apply to works made for hire. 17 U.S.C. § 304(d).

(3) This additional termination opportunity does not apply to grants made by will. 17 U.S.C. § 304(d).

C. Testamentary and Intestate Disposition of Copyrights.

1. A copyright is a form of personal property. State courts, therefore, have exclusive jurisdiction to probate wills disposing of copyrights. In the absence of a will, the intestate succession law of the decedent's domicile will determine the disposition of the copyright which was vested in the decedent at her death. This is true of common law copyrights as well as statutory copyrights in their initial or renewal term of protection.

2. The statutory succession rules of § 304(a) apply only to renewal rights which had not vested at the time of the decedent's death. The Copyright Act preempts state laws concerning the testamentary or intestate dispositions of nonvested renewal rights. As a result, the decedent's legatees or next of kin acquire no rights in nonvested renewal rights, except to the extent such rights are granted by § 304(a).

VIII. <u>INFRINGEMENT</u>.

A. Procedural Considerations.

1. An owner of the copyright or an exclusive licensee has standing to sue for copyright infringement. A nonexclusive licensee does not have standing to sue. 17 U.S.C. § 501(b); <u>Gamma Audio & Video, Inc. v. Ean-Chea</u>, 11 F.3d 1106 (1st Cir. 1993).

a. A "beneficial owner" of an exclusive right under a copyright is entitled to sue for infringement. 17 U.S.C. § 501(b).

(1) A beneficial owner is one who has relinquished legal ownership in exchange for an economic interest in the exploitation of the copyright. *See* <u>Cortner v. Israel</u>, 732 F.2d 267 (2d Cir. 1984).

(2) A copyright co-owner which files a renewal of the copyright in its own name, takes legal title to the

renewal copyright as a constructive trustee on behalf of the non-renewing co-owner, who becomes a beneficial owner. *See* Selznick v. Turner Entertainment Co., 990 F. Supp. 1180 (C.D. Cal. 1997).

2. Federal district courts have exclusive original jurisdiction over actions that arise under the Copyright Act. 28 U.S.C. § 1338(a).

   a. An action "arises under" the Copyright Act if: 1) the complaint is for a remedy expressly granted by the Act; 2) the claim requires a construction of the Act; or 3) a distinctive policy of the Act requires that federal principles control the disposition of the claim. T.B. Harms Co. v. Eliscu, 339 F.2d 823, 828 (2d Cir. 1964), *cert. denied*, 381 U.S. 915 (1965).

   b. A lawsuit that contains a copyright infringement claim which is only incidental to the plaintiff's asserted contractual rights does not arise under the Copyright Act. Schoenberg v. Shapolsky Publishers, Inc., 971 F.2d 926 (2d Cir. 1992). *But see* Vestron, Inc v. Home Box Office Inc., 839 F.2d 1380 (9th Cir. 1988) (under the well-pleaded complaint rule, a complaint that makes out an infringement claim and seeks remedies expressly created by federal copyright law is sufficient to establish federal jurisdiction).

   c. Courts have offered conflicting rulings on the issue of whether federal courts have jurisdiction to determine copyright ownership. *Compare* Merchant v. Levy, 92 F.3d 51, 55-56 (2d Cir. 1996) (authorship determination is federal question) *and* Lombardi v. Suares, 923 F. Supp. 51, 53-54 (S.D.N.Y. 1996) (issue of joint authorship which requires a determination of the applicability of definitions contained in the Copyright Act is one of copyright law, not contract law) *and* EMSA Limited Partnership v. Lincoln, 691 So. 2d 547 (Fla. Ct. App. 1997) (state courts have no jurisdiction to determine copyright ownership in the case of a work made for hire) *with* Franklin v. Cannon Films, Inc., 654 F. Supp. 133, 134-35 (C.D. Cal. 1987) (federal courts have no jurisdiction when copyright ownership is the sole question for consideration).

d. State law governs construction of the assignment of royalty interests. Yount v. Acuff Rose-Opryland, 103 F.3d 830, 835 (9th Cir. 1996); Iza Music Corp. v. W & K Music Corp., 995 F. Supp. 417, 418 (S.D.N.Y. 1998) ("a joint author's right to an accounting is a creature of state law rather than of the Copyright Act").

3. Registration of the copyright with the Copyright Office is a prerequisite to bringing a suit for copyright infringement of a work created by a United States author. 17 U.S.C. § 411(a); Quintanilla v. Texas Television Inc., 139 F.3d 494, 500 (5th Cir. 1998).

   a. Where the application for copyright registration has been rejected by the Copyright Office, the copyright owner may sue for copyright infringement, provided that the Register of Copyrights has been notified of the lawsuit and given a copy of the complaint. 17 U.S.C. § 411(a).

4. United States Copyright Law has no application to infringements that occur wholly outside the United States. Subafilms, Ltd. v. MGM-Pathe Communications Co., 24 F.3d 1088 (9th Cir. 1994).

5. Any person or entity actively involved in the infringing activity is a possible defendant in an infringement action. This would include employers, employees, printers and television or motion picture producers.

   a. Copyright infringement is a strict liability tort, a defendant need not have intended the infringement to be held liable. *See* Playboy Enterprises, Inc. v. Frena, 839 F. Supp. 1552 (M.D. Fla. 1993) (computer bulletin board operator was found liable for the infringement of copyrighted photographs which were uploaded and downloaded on his bulletin board without his knowledge).

   b. A corporate officer who personally participates in infringing activity may be personally liable for the infringement. *See* Southern Bell Tel. & Tel. v. Associated Tel. Directory Publishers, 756 F.2d 801, 811 (11th Cir. 1985).

c. An Internet access provider has been found not to be a direct infringer of copyrighted works posted on the Internet as it did not take any affirmative action that directly resulted in copying. *See* Religious Technology Center v. Netcom On-Line Communication Services, Inc., 907 F. Supp. 1361, 1368 (N.D. Cal. 1995).

d. A co-owner of a copyright cannot be liable to another co-owner for infringement of the copyright. Oddo v. Ries, 743 F.2d 630, 632-33 (9th Cir. 1984).

e. Contrary to § 511 of the Copyright Act which permits copyright infringement actions against "[a]ny State, any instrumentality of a State, and any officer or employee of a State," state sovereign immunity under the Eleventh Amendment may preclude the filing of a copyright infringement action against a state entity in federal court. *See* Seminole Tribe of Florida v. Florida, 517 U.S. 44 (1995); Chavez v. Arte Publico Press, 139 F.3d 504 (5th Cir. 1998); Rodriguez v. Texas Commission on the Arts, 992 F. Supp. 876 (N.D. Tex. 1998) (Eleventh Amendment bars action against state agency under the Copyright Act).

6. Right to Trial by Jury.

   a. The Seventh Amendment provides a right to a jury trial on all issues pertinent to an award of actual or statutory damages under § 504 of the Copyright Act, including the amount itself. Feltner v. Columbia Pictures Television, Inc., 118 S. Ct. 1279 (1998).

7. An unsuccessful litigant may be required to post a bond for the costs and attorneys fees the successful litigant may incur on appeal. *See* Adsani v. Miller, 139 F.3d 67 (2d Cir. 1998).

B. Direct Infringement.

1. To establish a claim of copyright infringement, plaintiff must demonstrate (1) ownership of a valid copyright, and (2) violation of any of the exclusive rights of the copyright owner.

2. Copyright ownership of a valid copyright.

   a. Production of a copyright registration certificate is prima facie proof of the existence of a valid copyright if the owner of the copyright filed the registration before or within five years of the date of first publication. 17 U.S.C. § 410(c); Evans and Assocs. Inc. v. Continental Homes, Inc., 785 F.2d 897, 903 (11th Cir. 1986).

   b. Plaintiff's chain of title from the author is presumed by reason of the registration certificate where the plaintiff obtained an assignment of rights prior to registration. Marobie-FL, Inc. v. Nat'l Ass'n of Fire Equipment Distributors, 983 F. Supp. 1167, 1173 (N.D. Ill. 1997).

3. Violation of an exclusive right.

   a. Copyright infringement is proven when the plaintiff can demonstrate: copying (access and substantial similarity) of a substantial portion of the plaintiff's work which is protected by copyright without the defendant being able to successfully assert an affirmative defense.

      (1) Access.

         (a) Access can be proven by evidence that the defendant had actually read or heard or had knowledge of plaintiff's work, or had a reasonable opportunity to view or hear the plaintiff's work. Jason v. Fonda, 698 F.2d 966 (9th Cir. 1983) ("bare possibility" that the producers and broadcasters of the motion picture had access to the author's book was insufficient to prove access).

         i) The reasonable opportunity to view or hear the plaintiff's work may be established by showing a particular chain of events by which the alleged infringer might have gained access through an intermediary. *See* Towler v. Sayles, 76 F.3d 579, 583 (4th Cir. 1996) (court may infer that alleged infringer had a reasonable possibility of access if the author sent the copyrighted work to a third party intermediary who has a close relationship with the infringer, such as one who supervises or works in the same department as the infringer or who contributes creative ideas to the infringer); Moore v. Columbia Pictures Indus., Inc., 972 F.2d 939, 942 (8th Cir. 1992); Gaste v. Kaiserman, 863 F.2d 1061, 1067 (2d Cir. 1988). *But see*, Shaw v. Lindheim, 809 F. Supp. 1393 (C.D. Cal. 1992) (relationship between two "co-creators" of allegedly infringing television series held insufficient to prove access); Weygand v. CBS, Inc., Copyright L. Rep. (CCH) ¶27,660 (C.D. Cal. 1997) (access by producer not imputed to co-producer).

(b) Access may be presumed where the plaintiff's work has been widely distributed to the public. Bright Tunes Music Corp. v. Harrisongs Music, Ltd., 420 F. Supp. 177 (S.D.N.Y. 1976), *aff'd sub nom.* ABKCO Music, Inc. v. Harrisongs Music, Ltd., 722 F.2d 988 (2d Cir. 1983).

(c) Under the "inverse ratio rule" proof of access may be reduced upon a showing of striking similarity.

i) Some courts require that the plaintiff prove at a minimum that defendant had a reasonable "possibility" to view or hear plaintiff's work. *See, e.g.*, Selle v. Gibb, 741 F.2d 896 (7th Cir. 1984).

ii) Other courts hold that once striking similarity is shown, the trier of fact is permitted to infer access without any affirmative evidence. *See, e.g.*, Repp v. Webber, 132 F.3d 882, 890 (2d Cir. 1997) (where defendant's musical composition is so strikingly similar to plaintiff's composition as to preclude the possibility of independent creation, access may be inferred without direct proof); Sylvestre v. Oswald, Copyright L. Dec. (CCH) ¶27,120 (S.D.N.Y. 1993).

iii) No amount of proof of access negates the need to prove substantial similarity. *See* Aliotti v. Dakin & Co., 831 F.2d 898, 902 (9th Cir. 1987).

(2) Distillation of copyrightable elements.

(a) In a copyright infringement action the court must distill the material in the plaintiff's work which is not protected by copyright, such as ideas, facts or non-original material, from the material in plaintiff's work which is protected by copyright. This latter material constitutes the only elements for which plaintiff may press her claim. *See* Computer Associates International, Inc. v. Altai, Inc., 982 F.2d 693 (2d Cir. 1992); Jarvis v. A & M Records, 827 F. Supp. 282, 291 (D.N.J. 1993) (because it is not unlawful to copy noncopyrightable portions of a plaintiff's work, noncopyrightable elements must be factored out in an inquiry into infringement).

(3) Substantial similarity.

(a) There is substantial similarity between the defendant's infringing work and the plaintiff's protected work where "the ordinary observer, unless he set out to detect the disparities, would be disposed to overlook them, and regard their aesthetic appeal as the same." Peter Pan Fabrics, Inc. v. Martin Weiner Corp., 274 F.2d 487, 489 (2d

Cir. 1960); Warner Brothers. v. American Broadcasting Companies, 654 F.2d 204 (2d Cir. 1981).

(b) The focus is on the similarities between the plaintiff's and defendant's works. *See* Sheldon v. Metro-Goldwyn Pictures Corp., 81 F.2d 49, 56 (2d Cir. 1936) ("[N]o plagiarist can excuse the wrong by showing how much of his work he did not pirate.").

(c) The Ninth Circuit utilizes an extrinsic and intrinsic test to determine infringement. *See* Sid & Marty Krofft Television Productions, Inc. v. McDonald's Corp., 562 F.2d 1157 (9th Cir. 1977).

i) Under the extrinsic test an objective comparative analysis is made between the copyrightable elements of the plaintiff's works and the defendant's work.

a) For literary works, those elements are: plot, theme, dialogue, mood, setting, pace, sequence of events and characters. Shaw v. Lindheim, 908 F.2d 531 (9th Cir. 1990).

b) For representational objects, those elements are: the type of artwork involved, the materials used, the subject matter and the setting for the subject. Sid & Marty Krofft Television Productions, Inc. v. McDonald's Corp., 562 F.2d 1157 (9th Cir. 1977).

ii) Under the intrinsic test a subjective comparative analysis utilizing a "total concept and feel" approach is called for. Shaw v. Lindheim, 908 F.2d 531 (9th Cir. 1990). The intrinsic test apparently takes the place of, or is equivalent to, the traditional substantial taking requirement.

(d) Other courts apply the gestalt-like "total concept and feel" analysis.

i) The Second Circuit takes the position that the total concept and feel analysis, rather than the traditional specific inquiry into plot and character development, is especially appropriate in an infringement action involving children's works, because "children's works are often less complex than those aimed at an adult audience." Williams v. Crichton, 84 F.3d 589 (2d Cir. 1996).

ii) Some courts apply the "total concept and feel" analysis without first distilling the copyrightable elements from the plaintiff's work. *See* Steinberg v. Columbia Pictures Industries, Inc., 663 F. Supp. 706 (S.D.N.Y. 1987). This approach can be criticized for its inclusion of noncopyrightable elements in its comparison of the works at issue.

(4) Substantial taking.

(a) Not every instance of copying constitutes actionable infringement. The copying must be substantial and material, either quantitatively or qualitatively, to constitute an infringement. *See* Arnstein v. Porter, 154 F.2d 464, 468-69 (2d Cir. 1946), *cert. denied*, 330 U.S. 851 (1947).

(b) A de minimis use of copyrighted material does not constitute an infringement. *See* Sandoval v. New Line Cinema Corp., 147 F.3d 215, 217 (2d Cir. 1998) (unauthorized use of photographs in motion picture *Seven* did not constitute infringement where they appeared fleetingly, were obscured, severely out of focus and virtually unidentifiable); Ringgold v. Black Entertainment Television, 126 F.3d 70, 76 (2d Cir. 1997) (where "the allegedly infringing work makes such a quantitatively insubstantial use of the copyrighted work as to fall below the threshold required for actionable copying, it makes more sense to reject the claim on that basis and find no infringement, rather than undertake an elaborate fair use analysis. . . .").

(5) Determination of the number of works involved.

(a) In a copyright infringement action the court must determine the work or number of works at issue. *See, e.g.*, Columbia Pictures Television v. Krypton Broadcasting of Birmingham, Inc., 106 F.3d 284, 293 (9th Cir. 1997), *rev'd on other grounds*, 118 S. Ct. 1279 (1998) (each episode of television series constitutes a separate copyrighted work); Triangle Publications, Inc. v. Knight-Ridder Newspapers, Inc., 626 F.2d 1171 (5th Cir. 1980) (work at issue was the cover of the T.V. Guide, not the entire magazine).

b. Unconscious infringement.

(1) The fact that a person innocently infringed a work protected by copyright does not preclude a finding of liability. Bright Tunes Music Corp. v. Harrisongs Music, Ltd., 420 F. Supp. 177 (S.D.N.Y. 1976), *aff'd sub nom.* ABKCO Music, Inc. v. Harrisongs Music, Ltd., 722 F.2d 988 (2d Cir. 1983); Sheldon v. Metro-Goldwyn Pictures Corp., 81 F.2d 49, 54 (2d Cir. 1936). Copyright infringement is a strict liability tort.

4. Elements of copyright infringement by unauthorized public performance, Almo Music Corp. v. 77 East Adam, Inc., 647 F. Supp. 123, 124 (N.D. Ill. 1986):

a. Originality and authorship of the compositions involved.

b. Compliance with the formalities required to secure a copyright.

c. Plaintiff's ownership of the copyrights of the relevant compositions.

d. Defendant's public performance of the compositions.

e. Defendant's failure to obtain permission from the plaintiff or its representatives for such performance.

C. Indirect Infringement.

1. Contributory Infringement.

a. An action for contributory infringement is not available without an underlying act of direct infringement. *See* DSC Communications Corp. v. Pulse Communications, Inc., 170 F.3d 1354, 1359 (Fed. Cir. 1999); Subafilms Ltd. v. MGM-Pathe Communications Co., 24 F.3d 1088, 1092 (9th Cir. 1994).

b. One who, with knowledge of the infringing activity, induces, causes or materially contributes to the infringing conduct of another may be liable in an infringement action. Gershwin Publishing Corp. v. Columbia Artists Management, Inc., 443 F.2d 1159 (1971).

c. An Internet access provider may be a contributory infringer for the infringing activity of its subscriber once the provider has been put on notice of the infringing activity. *See* Religious Technology Center v. Netcom On-Line Communication Services, Inc., 907 F. Supp. 1361, 1373 (N.D. Cal. 1995).

d. Swap Meet Cases.

(1) An operator of a swap meet who was aware that vendors renting booth space were selling counterfeit sound recordings was found to have materially contributed to the infringing conduct of the vendors by providing them with space, utilities, parking, advertising, plumber and customers. In addition, the operator protected the identity of infringers by not sharing such information with law enforcement, which the operator had earlier agreed to do. Fonovisa, Inc. v. Cherry Auction, Inc., 76 F.3d 259 (9th Cir. 1996).

2. Vicarious Infringement.

   a. Vicarious liability can be imposed when a party has the right and ability to supervise the infringing activity and also has a direct financial interest in such activities. Shapiro, Bernstein & Co., Inc. v. H.L. Green Co., Inc., 316 F.2d 304 (2d Cir. 1963). *See* All Nations Music v. Christian Family Network, Inc., 989 F. Supp. 863, 868-69 (W.D. Mich. 1997) (president of corporation that owned infringing radio station held to be vicariously liable). *But see* Religious Technology Center v. Netcom On-Line Communication Services, Inc., 907 F. Supp. 1361, 1375 (N.D. Cal. 1995) (Internet access provider not vicariously liable as it did not receive direct financial benefit from infringing activity of subscriber).

   b. Trade Show Cases.

      (1) *Compare* Polygram Int'l Publishing v. Nevada/TIG, Inc., 855 F. Supp. 1314 (D. Mass. 1994) (trade show organizer, found to have the ability to supervise the infringing activity of exhibitors and a direct financial interest in those activities, held to be an infringer) *with* Artists Music, Inc. v. Reed Publishing, Inc., 31 U.S.P.Q. 2d 1623 (S.D.N.Y. 1994) (trade show organizer, found to lack the ability to supervise the unauthorized performances of plaintiff's musical compositions and to not derive financial benefit from those performances, held not to be an infringer).

   c. Swap Meet Cases.

      (1) In Fonovisa, Inc. v. Cherry Auction, Inc., 76 F.3d 259 (9th Cir. 1996), the operator of a swap meet which had the right to terminate vendors who rented space, promoted the swap meet and controlled customer access was held to have sufficient ability to control the activities of the vendors who were selling counterfeit sound recordings at the swap meet. The operator was deemed to have received sufficient financial benefit through rental and admission

fees, as well as incidental payments for parking and food, even though the operator did not receive a commission tied to the sale of infringing items. The sale of pirated sound recordings at the swap meet was deemed a "draw" for customers, thereby benefitting the swap meet operator.

3. Limitations on Online Service Provider's Liability. 17 U.S.C. § 512.

   a. Broad definition of Online Service Provider (OSP). 17 U.S.C. § 512(k).

      (1) "Service Provider" is defined broadly as "a provider of online services or network access, or the operator of facilities therefor" for provisions other than those dealing with transitory digital network communications. This definition could include companies that maintain an Intranet for its employees or a bulletin board for customer comments.

   b. Eligibility. 17 U.S.C. § 512(i).

      (1) Limitations on online service provider's liability are available only if the OSP:

         (a) has adopted and reasonably implemented, and informs subscribers of, a policy that provides for termination of repeat infringers; and

         (b) accommodates and does not interfere with standard technical measures.

   c. Availability of Safe Harbors.

      (1) Transitory Digital Network Communications. 17 U.S.C. § 512(a).

         (a) Where the service provider is acting as a mere conduit it cannot be held liable for monetary relief.

         (b) Service provider can be enjoined from providing access to an identified subscriber or account holder who is using the provider's service to engage in infringing activity, as well as an online location outside the United States. 17 U.S.C. § 512(j).

(2) System Caching. 17 U.S.C. § 512(b).

(a) Where the service provider provides intermediate and temporary automatic storage of material made available online by a person other than the service provider, the service provider cannot be held liable for monetary relief.

(b) Service provider can be enjoined from providing access to an identified subscriber or account holder who is using the provider's service to engage in infringing activity, as well as an online location outside the United States. 17 U.S.C. § 512(j).

(3) Information Residing on Systems or Networks at Direction of Users. 17 U.S.C. § 512(c).

(a) Where the service provider provides storage of material at the direction of a user that resides on a system or network controlled or operated by the service provider, the service provider cannot be held liable for monetary relief if:

i) it does not have actual knowledge of the infringement; is not aware of facts or circumstances from which infringing activity is apparent; or acts expeditiously to remove, or disable access to infringing material, upon obtaining such knowledge or awareness;

ii) it does not receive a financial benefit directly attributable to the infringing activity; and

iii) upon notification of a claimed infringement responds expeditiously to remove, or disable access to the infringing material.

a) The OSP must designate an agent to receive notifications of claimed infringements. 17 U.S.C. § 512(c)(2).

b) Written notification of the claimed infringement must be provided to the designated agent. 17 U.S.C. § 512(c)(3).

(b) Service provider can be enjoined from providing access to an identified subscriber or account holder who is using the provider's service to engage in infringing activity, as well as an online location outside the United States. 17 U.S.C. § 512(j).

(4) Information Location Tools. 17 U.S.C. § 512(d).

(a) Where the service provider provides references or links to an online location containing infringing material by using information location tools, the service provider cannot be held liable for monetary relief if:

i) it does not have actual knowledge of the infringement; is not aware of facts or circumstances from which infringing activity is apparent; or acts expeditiously to remove, or disable access to infringing material, upon obtaining such knowledge or awareness;

ii) it does not receive a financial benefit directly attributable to the infringing activity; and

iii) upon notification of a claimed infringement responds expeditiously to remove, or disable access to the infringing material.

a) The OSP must designate an agent to receive notifications of claimed infringements.

b) Written notification of the claimed infringement and the identification of the reference or link must be provided to the designated agent. 17 U.S.C. § 512(d)(3).

(b) Service provider can be enjoined from providing access to an identified subscriber or account holder who is using the provider's service to engage in infringing activity, as well as an online location outside the United States. 17 U.S.C. § 512(j).

d. Notice and Put-Back Provisions. 17 U.S.C. § 512(g).

(1) When the OSP has removed or blocked material pursuant to the notice and take-down provisions, the OSP must:

(a) Take reasonable steps to promptly notify the subscriber that it has removed or disabled access to the allegedly infringing material;

(b) Upon receipt of a counter notification, promptly provide the copyright owner with a copy of the counter notification and inform the copyright owner that the OSP will replace the removed material or cease disabling access to it in 10 business days;

i) A counter notification is a written communication sent by the subscriber to the OSP's designated agent that identifies the material that was removed or disabled, states under penalty of perjury that the subscriber has a good faith belief that the removal or disabling was the result of mistake or misidentification, and consents to jurisdiction.

(c) Replace the removed material and cease disabling access to it not less than 10, nor more than 14, business days following receipt of the counter notice, unless its designated agent first receives notice that the copyright owner has filed an action seeking a court order to restrain the subscriber from engaging in the alleged infringing activity.

e. Subpoena to Identify Infringer. 17 U.S.C. § 512(h).

(1) A copyright owner may request the clerk of any United States district court to issue a subpoena to a service provider for identification of an alleged infringer.

4. Staple Article of Commerce Defense.

a. The manufacturer or distributor of a product capable of substantial noninfringing uses will not be liable for indirect copyright infringement. *See* Sony Corp. of America v. Universal City Studios, Inc., 464 U.S. 417 (1984) (video cassette recorder found capable of substantial noninfringing uses such as private, noncommercial time-shifting in the home).

D. Criminal Copyright Infringement.

1. Criminal liability may attach where a person "infringes a copyright willfully and for purposes of commercial advantage or private financial gain ... or by the reproduction or distribution ... of 1 or more copies or phonorecords of 1 or more copyrighted works, which have a total retail value of more than $1,000...." 17 U.S.C. § 506(a). *See generally* Saunders, *Criminal Copyright Infringement and the Copyright Felony Act*, 71 Denver. U.L. Rev. 671 (1994).

a. "Financial gain" includes the receipt, or expectation of receipt, of anything of value, including the receipt of other copyrighted works. 17 U.S.C. § 101 (definition of "financial gain").

2. Penalties for criminal copyright infringement, which may be deemed a felony, include up to six years in prison and heavy monetary fines. *See* 18 U.S.C. § 2319.

3. The statute of limitations for criminal copyright infringement is five years. 17 U.S.C. § 507(a).

E. Fair Use Defense.

1. Fair Use is a Judicially Created Doctrine.

a. "Fair use ... is 'a privilege in others than the owner of the copyright to use the copyrighted material in a reasonable manner without his consent.'" Harper & Row, Publishers, Inc. v. Nation Enterprises, 471 U.S. 539, 549 (1985) (quoting H. Ball, Law of Copyright and Literary Property 260 (1944)). *See generally* L. Seltzer, Exemptions and Fair Use in Copyright (1978); W. Patry, The Fair Use Privilege in Copyright Law (2d ed.1995).

b. As an affirmative defense, the defendant has the burden of proving the use was fair.

c. Fair use is an equitable rule of reason. H.R. Rep. No. 1476, 94th Cong., 2d Sess., at 65 (1976).

   (1) The primary inquiry is whether the defendant's work supersedes the use of the original work. *See* Folsom v. Marsh, 9 F. Cas. 342 (1841).

   (2) The fair use doctrine is based upon the balancing of the competing interests of the author, who has an economic incentive and seeks protection against unauthorized appropriations of her work; and society, which favors unhindered access to intellectual products.

d. "Take not from others to such an extent and in such a manner that you would be resentful if they so took from you." McDonald, *Non-infringing Uses*, 9 Bull. Cr. Soc'y 466, 467 (1962).

e. The purpose of the fair use doctrine is, in part, to facilitate the creation of additional works. "The fair use doctrine thus 'permits [and requires] courts to avoid rigid application of the copyright statute when, on occasion, it would stifle the very creativity which that law is designed to foster.'" Campbell v. Acuff-Rose Music, Inc., 510 U.S. 569, 577 (1994).

2. Fair Use Only Arises as a Defense to Copyright Infringement.

   a. It does not deal with the use of ideas.

   b. It does not deal with the use of facts.

c. It does not deal with an insubstantial taking. *See* Ringgold v. Black Entertainment Television, Inc., 126 F.3d 70, 76 (2d Cir. 1997).

3. Fair Use Doctrine is Codified at 17 U.S.C. § 107.

a. Section 107 codifies the factors developed under the prior case law. Marcus v. Rowley, 695 F.2d 1171 (9th Cir. 1983).

b. It was not the intent of Congress to freeze the fair use doctrine. H.R. Rep. No. 1476, 94th Cong., 2d Sess., at 66 (1976).

c. The preamble to § 107 lists several purposes, criticism, comment, news reporting, teaching, scholarship and research, which are examples of the sorts of uses likely to qualify as fair uses. Pacific & Southern Co., Inc. v. Duncan, 744 F.2d 1490 (11th Cir. 1984), *cert. denied*, 471 U.S. 1004 (1985). The uses listed are illustrative only. *See* Ringgold v. Black Entertainment Television, Inc., 126 F.3d 70, 78 (2d Cir. 1997). They are not determinative, nor do they constitute some type of threshold issue. The preamble provides "only general guidance about the sorts of copying that courts and Congress most commonly had found to be fair uses." Campbell v. Acuff-Rose Music, Inc., 510 U.S. 569, 577 (1994).

d. The four statutory nonexclusive factors are to be used by a court in determining the applicability of a fair use defense. Harper & Row, Publishers, Inc. v. Nation Enterprises, 471 U.S. 539, 560 (1985).

(1) Although the four factors are individually analyzed, they are interrelated. *See* Campbell v. Acuff-Rose Music, Inc., 510 U.S. 569 (1994).

(2) Each case raising the question of fair use must be decided on its own facts. "[T]he endless variety of situations and combinations of circumstances that can [a]rise in particular cases precludes the formulation of exact rules in the statute." H.R. Rep. No. 1476, 94th Cong., 2d Sess., at 66 (1976).

4. The Fair Use Factors.

   a. The purpose and character of the defendant's use.

      (1) A primary concern under this factor is whether the infringing work is transformative or does it merely supersede the need or the market for the original. *See* Castle Rock Entertainment, Inc. v. Carol Publishing Group, Inc., 150 F.3d 132, 142-43 (2d Cir. 1998) (book containing trivia questions about copyrighted television program not sufficiently transformative).

         (a) A transformative work is one which "adds something new, with a further purpose or different character, altering the first with new expression, meaning, or message...." Campbell v. Acuff-Rose Music, Inc., 510 U.S. 569, 579 (1994).

            i) Whether the defendant has made a productive use of the plaintiff's work may be helpful in calibrating the fair use balance. Sony Corp. v. Universal City Studios, Inc., 464 U.S. 417, 455 n.40 (1984). *See* Castle Rock Entertainment, Inc. v. Carol Publishing Group, Inc., 150 F.3d 132, 143 (2d Cir. 1998) (book containing trivia questions about *Seinfeld* television series had "little, if any, transformative purpose"); Twin Peaks Productions, Inc. v. Publications Int'l, Inc., 996 F.2d 1366 (2d Cir. 1993) (Defendant's summaries of episodes of plaintiff's television series was found to have no transformative function and was held to be an infringement); Los Angeles News Service v. KCAL-TV Channel 9, 108 F.3d 1119 (9th Cir. 1997) (broadcaster's voice-over did not add anything transformative to the plaintiff's videotape recording of Reginald Denny beating); Los Angeles News Service v. Reuters Television International Limited, 149 F.3d 987,

993 (9th Cir. 1998) (merely copying footage of the Los Angeles riots and transmitting it to news reporting organizations without explaining the footage, editing the content of the footage, or including editorial comment was not a transformative use).

ii) The more transformative the new work, the less significant other factors, such as commercialism, that may weigh against a finding of fair use. Campbell v. Acuff-Rose Music, Inc., 510 U.S. 569, 579 (1994); American Geophysical Union v. Texaco, Inc., 37 F.3d 881 (2d Cir. 1994) (unauthorized copying of scientific journals was non-transformative library building which was not entitled to fair use protection).

iii) A transformative use is not absolutely necessary for a finding of fair use. Sony Corp. v. Universal City Studios, Inc., 464 U.S. 417, 455 n.40 (1984).

(b) The greater the risk of market substitution, for the original work or its licensed derivatives, posed by the infringing work, the less likely it will be found to constitute a fair use. Campbell v. Acuff-Rose Music, Inc., 510 U.S. 569, 581 n.14 (1994).

i) A finding that the defendant copied the plaintiff's material to use it for the same intrinsic purpose for which the copyright owner intended it to be used is strong indicia of no fair use. Jartech, Inc. v. Clancy, 666 F.2d 403 (9th Cir. 1982). *See* Infinity Broadcasting Corp. v. Kirkwood, 150 F.3d 104, 108 (2d Cir. 1998) (use of infringed radio broadcasts for information rather than entertainment tends to support fair use claim).

ii) The distribution of a work to a broadcaster may be deemed not to be fair use, even though the broadcaster may successfully claim a fair use of the work. *See* Los Angeles News Service v. Reuters Television Int'l, Limited, 149 F.3d 987, 994 (9th Cir. 1998) (television news agencies that gather and provide audiovisual news material to subscribers for an annual fee not protected by fair use defense); Los Angeles News Service v. Tullo, 973 F.2d 791, 799 (9th Cir. 1992) (video news clipping service not protected by fair use defense).

(2) Commercial nature of defendant's use of the plaintiff's work.

(a) The first factor includes an inquiry into whether the defendant's use is of a commercial nature or is for a nonprofit use. *See* Harper & Row, Publishers, Inc. v. Nation Enterprises, 471 U.S. 539, 562 (1985) ("The fact that a publication was commercial as opposed to nonprofit is a separate factor that tends to weigh against a finding of fair use"); Stewart v. Abend, 495 U.S. 207, 237 (1990) (re-release of motion picture constituted a commercial use); Leibovitz v. Paramount Pictures Corp., 137 F.3d 109, 113 (2d Cir. 1998) (use for commercial purposes tends to point against fair use); Martin Luther King, Jr. Center for Social Change Inc. v. American Heritage Products, Inc., 508 F. Supp. 854 (N.D. Ga. 1981).

(b) Although the United States Supreme Court stated in Sony Corp. v. Universal City Studios, Inc., 464 U.S. 417, 451 (1984), that "every commercial use of copyrighted material is presumptively an unfair exploitation of the monopoly privilege that belongs to the owner of the copyright," the Court recently has retreated from this strongly stated position. The mere fact that a use is commercial does not bar a finding of fair use. Campbell v. Acuff-Rose Music, Inc., 510 U.S. 569, 583-84 (1994) (The only "presumption" of market harm supported by Sony would apply in a case involving mere duplication for commercial purposes). The mere fact that a copyright user is a commercial enterprise will not preclude the applicability of the fair use defense. *See* Warner Bros., Inc. v. American Broadcasting Companies, Inc., 523 F. Supp. 611 (S.D.N.Y. 1981), *aff'd*, 654 F.2d 204 (2d Cir. 1981).

(c) Profit-making institutions are presumed to be capable of negotiating and paying the copyright holder a fair fee for the use of the protected work. *See* Association of American Medical Colleges v. Mikaelian, 571 F. Supp. 144 (E.D. Pa.), *aff'd*, 734 F.2d 3 (3d Cir. 1983); Iowa State University Research Foundation, Inc. v. American Broadcasting Companies, Inc., 621 F.2d 57 (2d Cir. 1980) (fair use defense "is not a license for corporate theft").

(d) The fact that a charge is made for a work, or that a profit is anticipated does not convert the use into a commercial use. *See* Wright v. Warner Books, Inc., 953 F.2d 731, 736-37 (2d Cir. 1991); Higgins v. Detroit Education Television Foundation, 4 F. Supp. 2d 701, 705 (E.D. Mich. 1998).

(e) Unauthorized copying in the context of fund-raising efforts by non-profit organizations should be regarded in the same light as non-commercial uses. Hustler Magazine v. Moral Majority, Inc., 606 F. Supp. 1526, 1534-35 n.1 (C.D. Cal. 1985), *aff'd on other grounds*, 796 F.2d 1148 (9th Cir. 1986).

(f) The fact that a nonprofit organization is making a clearly educational use of copyrighted works is not, in and of itself, sufficient to sustain a fair use defense. *See e.g.* Encyclopedia Britannica Educational Corp. v. Crooks, 447 F. Supp. 243 (W.D.N.Y. 1978).

(3) Propriety of the defendant's conduct.

(a) The propriety of the defendant's conduct is relevant to the character of the defendant's use. Harper & Row, Publishers, Inc. v. Nation Enterprises, 471 U.S. 539, 562 (1985) (knowing exploitation of purloined manuscript); Fisher v. Dees, 794 F.2d 432, 437 (9th Cir. 1986); Los Angeles News Service v. KCAL-TV Channel 9, 108 F.3d 1119 (9th Cir. 1997) (use of videotape of Reginald Denny beating without attribution and with the broadcaster's logo superimposed on the footage were indications of bad faith).

(b) Although some courts have penalized defendants who proceed to use the plaintiff's work after their request for a license had been denied, the Supreme Court in Campbell found that being denied permission to use a work does not weigh against a finding of fair use. Campbell v. Acuff-Rose Music, Inc., 510 U.S. 569, 585 n.18 (1994).

(c) Some courts have been improperly influenced by their perception of the defendant or the defendant's work in determining whether a fair use defense should be recognized in a particular case. *See e.g.* MCA, Inc. v. Wilson, 677 F.2d 180 (2d Cir. 1981) ("We are not prepared to hold that a commercial composer can plagiarize a competitor's copyrighted song, substitute dirty lyrics of his own, perform it for commercial gain, and then escape liability by calling the end result a parody or satire on the mores of society"); Walt Disney Productions v. Mature Pictures Corp., 389 F. Supp. 1397, 1398 (S.D.N.Y. 1975) ("While defendants may have been seeking in their display of bestiality to parody life, they did not parody the Mickey Mouse March but sought only to improperly use the copyrighted material"). This approach recently has been discredited by the Supreme Court: "Whether... parody is in good taste or bad does not and should not matter to fair use." Campbell v. Acuff-Rose Music, Inc., 510 U.S. 569, 582-83 (1994).

(d) At least one court has argued that an obscene use is not a fair use. *See* Fisher v. Dees, 794 F.2d 432, 437 (9th Cir. 1986); *but see* Pillsbury Co. v. Milky Way Productions, Inc., 215 U.S.P.Q. 124, 131 & n.10 (N.D. Ga. 1981). This notion is contrary to rule that copyright law is not to be used to enforce the obscenity laws. *See* Mitchell Brothers Film Group v. Cinema Adult Theater, 604 F.2d 852 (5th Cir. 1979), *cert. denied*, 445 U.S. 917 (1980); Jartech, Inc. v. Clancy, 666 F.2d 403 (9th Cir. 1982).

b. The nature of the plaintiff's copyrighted work.

(1) The scope of fair use is greater when the plaintiff's work constitutes an informational type work, as opposed to a more creative product. Marcus v. Rowley, 695 F.2d 1171 (9th Cir. 1983). *See* Stewart v. Abend, 495 U.S. 207, 237-38 (1990) ("fair use is more likely to be found in factual works than in fictional works"); Harper & Row, Publishers, Inc. v. Nation Enterprises, 471 U.S. 539, 563 (1985) ("The law generally recognizes a greater need to disseminate factual works than works of fiction or fantasy"); Consumers Union of United States, Inc. v. General Signal Corp., 724 F.2d 1044, 1050 (2d Cir. 1983), *cert. denied*, 469 U.S. 823 (1984); Playboy v. Frena, 839 F. Supp. 1552, 1558 (M.D. Fla. 1993) (photographs of women are "in the category of fantasy & entertainment").

(a) News articles are deemed less close to the core of intended copyright protection than fictional pieces.

See Nihon Keizai Shimbun, Inc. v. Comline Business Data, Inc., 166 F.3d 65, 72 (2d Cir. 1999).

(2) An additional concern is "[w]hether the original is creative, imaginative, or represents an investment of time in anticipation of a financial return...." Rogers v. Koons, 960 F.2d 301, 310 (2d Cir.), *cert. denied*, 506 U.S. 934 (1992).

(3) Unpublished works.

(a) Fair use traditionally was not recognized as a defense to charges of copying from an author's as yet unpublished works. Harper & Row, Publishers, Inc. v. Nation Enterprises, 471 U.S. 539, 550-55 (1985). "The unpublished nature of a work is a key, though not necessarily determinative, factor tending to negate a defense of fair use." Harper & Row, Publishers, Inc. v. Nation Enterprises, 471 U.S. 539, 554 (1985) (quoting W. Patry, The Fair Use Privilege in Copyright Law 125 (1985)). *See* Sundeman v. The Seajay Society, Inc., 142 F.3d 194, 203-04 (4th Cir. 1998); Salinger v. Random House, Inc., 818 F.2d 252 (2d Cir. 1987).

(b) To clarify the rule that a fair use may be found even though the plaintiff's work is unpublished, § 107 was amended in 1992. The following sentence was added: "The fact that a work is unpublished shall not itself bar a finding of fair use if such finding is made upon consideration of all the above factors." 17 U.S.C. § 107. *See* Sundeman v. The Seajay Society, Inc., 142 F.3d 194, 204-05 (4th Cir. 1998).

(4) The fact that the plaintiff's work is out of print and, therefore, not available to the public, supports a finding of fair use. Maxtone-Graham v. Burtchaell, 803 F.2d 1253 (2d Cir. 1986); Duffy v. Penguin Books USA Inc., 4 F. Supp. 2d 268, 274 (S.D.N.Y. 1998); *compare* Craft v. Kobler, 667 F. Supp. 120 (S.D.N.Y. 1987) (fact that plaintiff's books on

Stravinsky are out of print is not determinative on the issue of fair use).

c. The amount and substantiality of the portion used.

(1) This factor requires an analysis of both the quantity and quality of the alleged infringement. Marcus v. Rowley, 695 F.2d 1171 (9th Cir. 1983); Salinger v. Random House, Inc., 818 F.2d 252 (2d Cir. 1987).

(a) Use of the "heart" of the plaintiff's work reduces the likelihood that a fair use will be found. *See* Harper & Row Publishers, Inc. v. Nation Enter., 471 U.S. 539, 565-66 (1985) (discussion of Nixon pardon was "heart" of Gerald Ford's memoir); Los Angeles News Service v. Reuters Television Int'l, Limited, 149 F.3d 987, 994 (9th Cir. 1998).

i) The quoting of plaintiff's material is an indication that the material quoted is of significant value, but need not be the heart of the work. *See* Sundeman v. The Seajay Society, Inc., 142 F.3d 194, 205 (4th Cir. 1998).

(2) There are no absolute rules as to how much of a copyrighted work may be copied and still be considered a fair use. *See* Maxtone-Graham v. Burtchaell, 803 F.2d 1253, 1263 (2d Cir. 1986); Higgins v. Detroit Education Television Foundation, 4 F. Supp. 2d 701, 707 (E.D. Mich. 1998) (use of 35 seconds of musical composition, without lyrics, as background music in an educational television program held to be a fair use). The extent of permissible copying varies with the purpose and character of the use. Campbell v. Acuff-Rose Music, Inc., 510 U.S. 569, 579 (1994).

(3) The greater the amount of the copyrighted work used, the less likely it is that the fair use exception is applicable.

(a) A fair use defense is rarely viable where the defendant has made a verbatim or near-verbatim copy of the plaintiff's work. Benny v. Loew's, Inc., 239 F.2d 532 (9th Cir. 1956), *aff'd by an equally divided court*, 356 U.S. 43 (1958); Hustler Magazine, Inc. v. Moral Majority, Inc., 796 F.2d 1148 (9th Cir. 1986); Rosemont Enterprises, Inc. v. Random House, Inc., 366 F.2d 303, 316 (2d Cir. 1966), *cert. denied*, 385 U.S. 1009 (1967); Wihtol v. Crow, 309 F.2d 777 (9th Cir. 1962); Encyclopedia Britannica Educational Corp. v. Crooks, 447 F. Supp. 243 (W.D.N.Y. 1978).

(b) The fact that an entire work is reproduced by the defendant does not have its ordinary effect of militating against a finding of fair use when the viewer has been invited to witness the work in its entirety free of charge. Sony Corp. v. Universal City Studios, Inc., 464 U.S. 417, 449-50 (1984).

(c) The fact that a substantial portion of the infringing work was copied verbatim is evidence of the qualitative value of the copied material, both to the originator and to the plagiarist who seeks to profit from marketing someone else's copyrighted expression. Harper & Row, Publishers, Inc. v. Nation Enterprises, 471 U.S. 539, 565 (1985).

(d) A defendant may be permitted to take a greater amount of the copyrighted work where there is a special need for accuracy. *See* Meeropol v. Nizer, 560 F.2d 1061, 1071 (2d Cir.), *cert. denied*, 434 U.S. 1013 (1977); Walt Disney Productions v. Air Pirates, 581 F.2d 751, 756-57 (9th Cir. 1978). *But see* Salinger v. Random House, Inc., 818 F.2d 252 (2d Cir. 1987).

(4) The percentage of the infringing work which is directly copied from the plaintiff's work is also a relevant concern. Campbell v. Acuff-Rose Music, Inc., 510 U.S. 569, 586-87 (1994).

(a) Where the infringing work largely consists of the plaintiff's work, it demonstrates a dearth of transformative character, thus less likely to be considered a fair use under the first factor.

(b) Where the infringing work largely consists of the plaintiff's work, it presents a greater likelihood of market harm under the fourth factor.

d. The effect of the defendant's use upon the potential market for the plaintiff's copyrighted work.

(1) Although this factor was deemed "undoubtedly the single most important element of fair use" in Harper & Row, Publishers, Inc. v. Nation Enterprises, 471 U.S. 539, 566 (1985), the factor has become more relativistic after the Campbell decision. "Market harm is a matter of degree, and the importance of this factor will vary, not only with the amount of harm, but also with the relative strength of the showing on the other factors." Campbell v. Acuff-Rose Music, Inc., 510 U.S. 569, 590 n.21 (1994).

(2) A use of the protected work which destroys the value of the protected work to the copyright owner is not considered fair. *See* Meeropol v. Nizer, 560 F.2d 1061 (2d Cir.), *cert. denied*, 434 U.S. 1013 (1977); Sampson & Murdock Co. v. Seaver-Radford Co., 140 F. 539 (1st Cir. 1905); Elsmere Music, Inc. v. National Broadcasting Co., 482 F. Supp. 741, 747 (S.D.N.Y.), *aff'd*, 623 F.2d 252, 253 (2d Cir. 1980) (fair use allowed where defendant's song did not interfere with the marketability of plaintiff's song; where it did not affect the value of the plaintiff's song and where it did not have the effect of fulfilling the demand for the original); Los Angeles News Service v. KCAL-TV Channel 9, 108 F.3d 1119 (9th Cir. 1997) (use of videotape of news event by potential licensee was an injury to plaintiff's primary market).

(3) There need be no actual harm to the marketability of the plaintiff's work. The potential of such harm is also relevant.

(a) Courts are to look beyond the market harm caused by the particular actions of the defendant and decide whether unrestricted and widespread conduct of the sort engaged in by the defendant would result in a substantially adverse impact on the potential market for the original. Campbell v. Acuff-Rose Music, Inc., 510 U.S. 569, 590 (1994).

(b) The fact that the defendant is a competitor of the plaintiff makes a finding of fair use less likely. *See, e.g.*, Los Angeles News Service v. Reuters Television Int'l, Limited, 149 F.3d 987, 994 (9th Cir. 1998).

(c) Courts must also take into account the potential harm to the market for derivative works. Campbell v. Acuff-Rose Music, Inc., 510 U.S. 569, 590 (1994) ("the licensing of derivatives is an important economic incentive to the creation of originals.").

i) There is no protectible derivative market for criticism. *See* Campbell v. Acuff-Rose Music, Inc., 510 U.S. 569, 592 (1994); Sundeman v. The Seajay Society, Inc., 142 F.3d 194, 207 (4th Cir. 1998).

(d) The term "potential markets" includes only those markets that the copyright owner would ordinarily develop or license. Castle Rock Entertainment v. Carol Publishing Group, Inc., 150 F.3d 132, 145 (2d Cir. 1998).

(4) Where it is clear that the defendant's use has no effect on the potential market for the plaintiff's work, the fair use defense is likely to be upheld. *See* Sony Corp. v. Universal City Studios, Inc., 464 U.S. 417, 450 (1984); Keep Thompson Governor Com-

mittee v. Citizens for Gallen, 457 F. Supp. 957 (D.N.H. 1978); Jacobson, "Fair Use: Considerations in Written Works," 2 Comm. & the Law 17, 30 (1980). *But see* Salinger v. Random House, Inc., 818 F.2d 252 (2d Cir. 1987) (fact that plaintiff had disavowed any intention to publish works during his lifetime does not prohibit a finding of fair use).

e. Some courts have added a fifth factor to the fair use analysis, that of the public interest. *See* Rosemont Enterprises, Inc. v. Random House, Inc., 366 F.2d 303 (2d Cir. 1966); Time, Inc. v. Bernard Geis Associates, 293 F. Supp. 130 (S.D.N.Y. 1968); Hustler Magazine v. Moral Majority, Inc., 606 F. Supp. 1526, 1536 (C.D. Cal. 1985), *aff'd*, 796 F.2d 1148 (9th Cir. 1986); National Rifle Assoc. of America v. Handgun Control Federation, 15 F.3d 559, 562 (6th Cir. 1994) ("The scope of the fair use doctrine is wider when the use relates to issues of public concern.). This approach was rejected in Walt Disney Productions v. Air Pirates, 581 F.2d 751, 759 (9th Cir. 1978).

5. Special Applications of the Fair Use Doctrine.

a. Scholarly Use.

(1) The quotation of short passages in a scholarly or technical work, for purposes of illustration or clarification of the author's observations traditionally has been protected by fair use. H.R. Rep. No. 1476, 94th Cong., 2d Sess., at 65 (1976). *See* Meeropol v. Nizer, 560 F.2d 1061 (2d Cir.), *cert. denied*, 434 U.S. 1013 (1977) (in determining the applicability of fair use it is relevant whether or not the Rosenberg letters were used primarily for scholarly, historical reasons, or predominantly for commercial exploitation); Harper & Row, Publishers, Inc. v. Nation Enterprises, 471 U.S. 539, 563 (1985) ("Fair use distinguishes between a true scholar and a chiseler who infringes a work for personal profit"). *See*

generally Fair Use and Free Inquiry (J. Lawrence & B. Timberg, eds. 1980).

(2) In determining fair use questions, the courts have placed particular emphasis on whether the use of the copyrighted work by the alleged infringer "would serve the public interest in the free dissemination of information and whether their preparation requires some use of prior materials dealing with the same subject matter. *See* Sundeman v. The Seajay Society, Inc., 142 F.3d 194, 203-04, 206 (4th Cir. 1998) ("It would severely restrict scholarly pursuit, and inhibit the purposes of the Copyright Act, if a fragile original could not be copied to facilitate literary criticism."); Rosemont Enterprises, Inc. v. Random House, Inc., 366 F.2d 303 (2d Cir. 1966).

b. Parody, Burlesque and Satire.

(1) The parody cases constitute a special application of the fair use defense, recognizing the need to protect this form of expression. See Fisher v. Dees, 794 F.2d 432, 435 (9th Cir. 1986). *Cf.* Hustler Magazine v. Falwell, 485 U.S. 46 (1988).

(2) Parody has an obvious claim to transformative value. As a form of comment or criticism, parody can provide social benefit by shedding light on an earlier work, and, in the process, creating a new work. Campbell v. Acuff-Rose Music, Inc., 510 U.S. 569, 579 (1994).

(a) The threshold question when fair use is raised in defense of parody is whether a parodic character may reasonably be perceived. Campbell v. Acuff-Rose Music, Inc., 510 U.S. 569, 582 (1994) (The Court did not address the issue of whether an intent to parody is required).

(b) In Campbell the Court drew a distinction between parody and satire. The Court viewed parody as an infringing work which targets the plaintiff's work, at least in part, as the object of the parody. *See* Leibovitz v. Paramount Pictures Corp., 137 F.3d 109 (2d Cir. 1998) (teaser ad for motion picture deemed a fair use as it targeted photograph of nude pregnant Demi Moore as an object of parody); Dr. Seuss Enterprises, L.P. v. Penguin Books USA, Inc., 109 F.3d 1394 (9th Cir. 1997) (defendant's work which mimicked Dr. Seuss' style, did not target it for comment or criticism, and therefore did not constitute a fair use). The Court viewed satire as a more generalized social commentary which uses the plaintiff's work merely as a vehicle. Although a work of satire could possibly make a successful claim of fair use, it is not deemed deserving of the special consideration given to parody. *See also* MCA, Inc. v. Wilson, 677 F.2d 180 (2d Cir. 1981); Columbia Pictures Industries, Inc. v. Miramax Films Corp., 11 F. Supp. 2d 1179, 1188 (C.D. Cal. 1998) ("Miramax has merely used [Columbia's poster] as a vehicle to poke fun at another target—corporate America. It has not used its advertising to comment on or criticize the copyrighted work.").

(3) The Supreme Court has found that only creative works serve as the targets of parody. As a result, the second fair use factor has little relevance when deciding whether a parody is to be protected as a fair use. Campbell v. Acuff-Rose Music, Inc., 510 U.S. 569, 586 (1994) (second factor not "likely to help much in separating the fair use sheep from the infringing goats in a parody case, since parodies almost invariably copy publicly known, expressive works.").

(4) The parodist is permitted to appropriate enough of the plaintiff's work to "conjure up" the object of the parody. Enough of the original may be taken "to make the object of its critical wit recognizable." Campbell v. Acuff-Rose Music, Inc., 510 U.S. 569, 588 (1994).

(a) The amount taken does not become excessive merely because the portion taken was the heart of the original.

(b) Once enough has been taken to assure identification, additional appropriation must be balanced against the extent of the parody, the amount of new material added by the defendant and the likelihood that the parody may serve as a market substitute for the original.

(c) In the area of parody, there are three considerations to be made in determining whether a taking is excessive under the circumstances: the degree of public recognition of the original work, the ease of conjuring up the original work in the chosen medium, and the focus of the parody. Fisher v. Dees, 794 F.2d 432, 439 (9th Cir. 1986) (a song is difficult to parody effectively without exact or near-exact copying).

(5) Where the defendant's work is a parody, it will not be protected by fair use if the parody has the effect of fulfilling the demand for the original. Berlin v. E.C. Publications, 329 F.2d 541 (2d Cir. 1964); Elsmere Music, Inc. v. NBC, 482 F. Supp. 741 (S.D.N.Y.), aff'd, 623 F.2d 252 (2d Cir. 1980).

(a) Market harm which may be caused by the lethal nature of biting criticism is not cognizable under the Copyright Act.

(b) There is no protectible derivative market for criticism such as parody.

i) Creators of imaginative works generally do not license critical reviews or lampoons of their own productions.

ii) The parody and the original usually serve different market functions.

(c) The Supreme Court in *Campbell* did not address what effect, if any, the defendant's intent to fulfill the demand for the original. *See* Berlin v. E.C. Publications, 329 F.2d 541 (2d Cir. 1964).

(6) The creator of the parody is not permitted to take as much of the plaintiff's work as he or she needs to make the "best parody." "Instead, their desire to make the 'best parody' is balanced against the rights of the copyright owner in his original expressions." Walt Disney Productions v. Air Pirates, 581 F.2d 751, 758 (9th Cir. 1978).

(7) Advertising parodies find it more difficult to assert a fair use claim. *See* Columbia Pictures Industries, Inc. v. Miramax Films Corp., 11 F. Supp. 2d 1179, 1187 (C.D. Cal. 1998) ("Advertisements are entitled to less indulgence than other forms of parody.").

c. Set Dressing.

(1) The use of artwork as a prop in a television program or motion picture constitutes an infringement where its use is more than de minimis. *See* Sandoval v. New Line Cinema Corp., 147 F.3d 215 (2d Cir. 1998).

(2) The shorter the period of time the artwork is depicted, the less recognizable the artwork in the program or film, and the less attention is drawn to the artwork in dialogue, action of the actors or camera focus, the greater the likelihood a fair use will be found. *See* Ringgold v. Black Entertainment Television, Inc., 126 F.3d 70 (2d Cir. 1997); Jackson v. Warner Bros., Inc., 993 F. Supp. 585 (E.D. Mich. 1997); Sandoval v. New Line Cinema Corp., 973 F. Supp. 409, *aff'd on other grounds*, 147 F.3d 215 (2d Cir. 1998).

d. Use of a Protected Work in Litigation.

(1) Use of a copyrighted photograph, admitted into evidence, in a criminal trial has been found to constitute a fair use. *See* Kulik Photography v. Cochran, 975 F. Supp. 812, 814 (E.D. Va. 1997).

e. Home Taping.

(1) Video taping of broadcast television programs, which the viewer has been invited to witness in its entirety free of charge, for purposes of private, non-commercial, time-shifting, is protected by fair use. Sony Corp. v. Universal City Studios, Inc., 464 U.S. 417 (1984).

(2) The Audio Home Recording Act now permits the private, noncommercial taping of both analog and digital sound recordings. *See* 17 U.S.C. § 1008.

f. Photocopying Materials.

(1) A detailed agreement on guidelines for classroom copying in not-for-profit educational institutions was entered into by interested parties at the time of the passage of the 1976 Copyright Act. This agreement was not intended to have the force of law. *See* Marcus v. Rowley, 695 F.2d 1171 (9th Cir. 1983); Addison-Wesley Publishing Co., Inc. v. New York University, 1983 Copyright L. Dec. (CCH) ¶25,544 (S.D.N.Y. 1983).

(2) Under this agreement:

(a) A teacher may make a single copy of a work for use in scholarly research or teaching.

(b) Multiple copies of a work may be made for classroom use provided that:

i) The copying meets the tests of brevity and spontaneity.

a) The test of brevity for prose allows for the reproduction of a complete work of fewer than 2,500 words or an excerpt of the work of not more than 1,000 words or 10% of the work, whichever is less.

b) The test of spontaneity allows for the reproduction of the work when the decision to use the work is so close in time to the moment of its use that it would be unreasonable to expect a timely reply to a request for permission to use it.

ii) Meets the cumulative effect test defined in the agreement.

a) The copying of the material is for only one course in the school in which the copies are made.

b) Not more than one complete work or two excerpts may be copied from the same author, nor more than three from the same collective work or periodical volume during one class term.

c) No more than nine instances of multiple copying is permitted for one course during one class term.

iii) Each copy includes a notice of copyright.

F. Other Affirmative Defenses.

1. Valid License.

a. The existence of a license, whether exclusive or nonexclusive in nature, creates an affirmative defense to a claim of copyright infringement. I.A.E., Inc. v. Shaver, 74 F.3d 768, 775 (7th Cir. 1996); Graham v. James, 144 F.3d 229, 236 (2d Cir. 1998) (copyright owner who grants nonexclusive license waives right to sue licensee for copyright infringement).

(1) The licensee has the burden of proving the existence of a license. Bourne v. Walt Disney Co., 68 F.3d 621 (2d Cir. 1995).

(2) Once the existence of a license has been proven, the copyright owner bears the burden of proving the scope of the license. S.O.S., Inc. v. Payday, Inc., 886 F.2d 1081, 1085 (9th Cir. 1989).

(a) Use of a copyrighted work in a manner or to an extent not authorized by the license constitutes copyright infringement. *See* Marshall v. New Kids on the Block, 780 F. Supp. 1005 (S.D.N.Y. 1991); Kanakos v. Mx Trading Corp., 216 U.S.P.Q. 1030 (S.D.N.Y. 1981).

(3) Continued use of a copyrighted work after the license has been terminated constitutes copyright infringement. *See* Powell v. Green Hill Publishers, Inc., 719 F. Supp. 743 (N.D. Ill. 1989) (continued publication of book following termination of license found to be copyright infringement).

b. An authorization to use a copyrighted work from one joint copyright owner is an effective defense to an infringement action brought by another joint owner. Lone Wolf McQuade Associates v. CBS, Inc., 961 F. Supp. 587 (S.D.N.Y. 1997); SBK Catalogue Partnership v. Orion Pictures Corp., 723 F. Supp. 1053, 1059 (D.N.J. 1989). *But see* Leichester v. Warner Bros., 47 U.S.P.Q.2d 1501 (C.D. Cal. 1998) (earlier infringement cannot be retroactively validated by later grant of license from joint owner).

2. First Amendment.

a. Several courts have addressed the issue of whether a defense based on the First Amendment, separate from the fair use defense, should be recognized. To date, no court has adopted such a defense, though a compelling set of facts may persuade a court of the need for such a defense. *See* Harper & Row, Publishers, Inc. v. Nation Enterprises, 471 U.S. 539 (1985) (idea/expression dichotomy of copyright law sufficiently balances the interests of the First Amendment and copyright); Dallas Cowboys Cheerleaders, Inc. v. Scoreboard Posters, Inc., 600 F.2d 1184 (5th Cir. 1979); Walt Disney Productions v. Air Pirates, 581 F.2d 751 (9th Cir. 1978); Triangle Publications, Inc. v. Knight-Ridder Newspapers, Inc., 626 F.2d 1171 (5th Cir. 1980); Urantia Foundation v. Maaherra, 895 F. Supp.

1329, 1333-34 (D. Ariz. 1995) (First Amendment defense would be limited to a graphic expression of news).

3. Statute of Limitations.

   a. There is a three year statute of limitations for copyright infringement actions. 17 U.S.C. § 507.

   b. The circuits are divided as to when the statute of limitations begins to run.

      (1) Some courts find that each act of infringement is a distinct harm giving rise to an independent claim for relief. Recovery is allowed only for those acts occurring within three years of the filing of the lawsuit, and is disallowed for earlier infringing acts. *See* Roley v. New World Pictures, Ltd., 19 F.3d 479 (9th Cir. 1994); Stone v. Williams, 970 F.2d 1043 (2d Cir. 1992); Hoste v. Radio Corp. of America, 654 F.2d 11 (6th Cir. 1981). *Cf.* Daboub v. Gibbons, 42 F.3d 285 (5th Cir. 1995) (statute of limitations began to run when alleged infringer "copyrighted the song" and that subsequent acts of infringement constituted continuing damages, rather than a continuing tort).

         (a) Claims of co-ownership, as distinct from claims of infringement, have been held to accrue when plain and express repudiation of co-ownership is communicated to the claimant, and are barred three years from the time of repudiation. *See* Zuill v. Shanahan, 80 F.3d 1366, 1369 (9th Cir. 1996).

      (2) Other courts have applied the continuing tort doctrine to copyright infringement cases, finding that only the last infringing act that constitutes a continuing tort need be within the statutory period. *See* Taylor v. Meirick, 712 F.2d 1112 (7th Cir. 1983); United States v. Shabazz, 724 F.2d 1536 (11th Cir. 1984).

4. Laches.

   a. The equitable defense of laches applies when there has been a sufficient passage of time between the plaintiff's knowledge of the injury and the date of bringing suit, and the presence of prejudice to the defendant. *See* Jackson v. Axton, 25 F.3d 884 (9th Cir. 1994) (musician's claim of coauthorship was barred by laches after waiting 22 years to assert claim).

5. Abandonment of Copyright.

   a. Abandonment of copyright occurs only if there is an intent by the copyright proprietor to surrender the rights in her work. An overt act evidencing such an intent is necessary. National Comics Publications, Inc. v. Fawcett Publications, Inc., 191 F.2d 594 (2d Cir. 1951).

   b. Abandonment of some rights by the copyright owner does not necessarily constitute an abandonment of all rights in the copyright. *See* Micro Star v. Formgen, Inc., 154 F.3d 1107, 1114 (9th Cir. 1998).

6. Copyright Misuse.

   a. A misuse of copyright has been found to occur when a copyright is being used in a manner violative of the public policy embodied in the grant of a copyright. *See, e.g.*, Alcatel USA, Inc. v. DGI Technologies, Inc., 166 F.3d 772, 792-93 (5th Cir. 1999) (use of copyright in software to indirectly gain commercial control over uncopyrighted hardware constitutes misuse); Practice Management Information Corp. v. American Medical Ass'n, 121 F.3d 516 (9th Cir. 1997); Lasercomb America, Inc. v. Reynolds, 911 F.2d 970, 978 (4th Cir. 1990); PRC Realty Systems, Inc. v. National Ass'n of Realtors, 1992 Copyright L. Dec. (CCH) ¶26,961 (4th Cir. 1992) (Unpublished Disposition).

   b. Misuse of a copyright, in violation of the antitrust laws, may be asserted as a defense to copyright infringement. Lasercomb America, Inc. v. Reynolds, 911 F.2d 970, 978 (4th Cir. 1990).

   c. Use of a copyright license to prohibit the independent implementation of ideas is adverse to the public policy embodied in copyright law.

(1) Use of a "no-contest" clause in a copyright licensing agreement is valid unless shown to violate antitrust law.

7. Fraud on the Copyright Office.

   a. A copyright owner's fraud or inequitable conduct in obtaining a federal registration may be a defense to a copyright infringement action.

   b. The misrepresentation or omission must be material and intentional.

8. Obscenity.

   a. Obscenity is not a defense to copyright infringement. The general rule is that copyright protection is to be accorded a work that has met the statutory prerequisites, even if it is obscene. *See* Mitchell Brothers Film Group v. Cinema Adult Theater, 604 F.2d 852 (5th Cir. 1979), *cert. denied*, 445 U.S. 917 (1980); Jartech, Inc. v. Clancy, 666 F.2d 403 (9th Cir. 1982). *But see* Devils Films, Inc. v. Nectar Video, 29 F. Supp. 2d 174 (S.D.N.Y. 1998) (court refused to exercise its equitable powers to enjoin the alleged infringement of plaintiff's films that the court found to be obscene).

9. Preemption. 17 U.S.C. § 301.

   a. Various state causes of action may be preempted by the federal copyright act. *See* Mayer v. Josiah Wedgwood & Sons, Ltd., 601 F. Supp. 1523 (S.D.N.Y. 1985). There are three requirements for § 301 preemption:

      (1) The cause of action must arise on or after January 1, 1978.

      (2) The subject matter of the suit must come within the subject matter of copyright as defined by §§ 102 & 103 of the 1976 Copyright Act.

         (a) The subject matter need not be actually protected by the Copyright Act, it need merely be the "type" of thing covered by the copyright laws. Synercom Technology, Inc. v. University Computing Co., 474 F. Supp. 37, 43 (N.D. Tex. 1979). *See* United States ex rel. Berge v. Board of Trustees of The University of Alabama, 104 F.3d 1453 (4th Cir. 1997) (Copyright Act's "scope" is broader than its "protection"). *But see* Allarcom Pay Television Ltd. v. General Instrument Corp., 69 F.3d 381 (9th Cir. 1995) (unauthorized satellite transmission did not constitute an act of copyright infringement within the United States, therefore state law claim not preempted).

(3) The right asserted must be equivalent to a right protected by federal copyright law. Vault Corp. v. Quaid Software, 847 F.2d 255 (5th Cir. 1988).

(a) In determining whether the state law claim asserts a right equivalent to a right protected by copyright law the courts use the "extra elements" test. Under this test, it is determined whether the state cause of action requires proof of an element that is qualitatively different from proof required for a showing of copyright infringement. *See* Daboub v. Gibbons, 42 F.3d 285, 288, 289-90 (5th Cir. 1995); Trandes Corp. v. Guy F. Atkinson Co., 996 F.2d 655, 659 (4th Cir. 1993); Valente-Kritzer Video v. Pinckney, 881 F.2d 772 (9th Cir. 1989), *cert. denied*, 493 U.S. 1062 (1990) (state fraud claim requirement of misrepresentation constituted an extra element).

b. A split of authority has emerged over the issue of whether "shrinkwrap" licenses, often used in connection with the sale of computer programs, are preempted. *Compare* ProCD, Inc. v. Zeidenberg, 86 F.3d 1447 (7th Cir. 1996) (such licenses not preempted) *with* Vault Corp. v. Quaid Software, 847 F.2d 255 (5th Cir. 1988) (such licenses are preempted).

c. An action for the violation of the right of publicity is generally deemed not to be preempted. *See* Waits v.

Frito-Lay, Inc., 978 F.2d 1093 (9th Cir. 1992) (tort of appropriation of voice is not preempted); Fleet v. CBS, Inc., 50 Cal. App. 4th 1911 (1996); *but see* Baltimore Orioles, Inc. v. Major League Baseball Players Ass'n, 805 F.2d 663 (7th Cir. 1986), *cert. denied*, 480 U.S. 941 (1987) (baseball players' right of publicity claim in their game performances held preempted); Ahn v. Midway Mfging Co., 965 F. Supp. 1134 (N.D. Ill. 1997) (right of publicity action brought by martial arts practitioner who modeled for the arcade version of video game held preempted).

d. The tort of misappropriation may be preempted. *See* Alcatel USA, Inc. v. DGI Technologies, Inc., 166 F.3d 772 (5th Cir. 1999); National Basketball Assoc. Inc. v. Motorola, Inc., 105 F.3d 841 (2d Cir. 1997) (only narrow "hot news" misappropriation claim survives preemption for actions concerning material within the realm of copyright).

e. Trade secret claims are generally not preempted due to the requirement of an additional element, breach of trust. *See* DSC Communications Corp. v. Pulse Communications, Inc., 170 F.3d 1354, 1365 (Fed. Cir. 1999) (additional element of misappropriation of information regulates conduct qualitatively different from that regulated by copyright law); Gates Rubber Co. v. Bando Chemical Indus., Ltd., 9 F.3d 823 (10th Cir. 1993). *But see* DSC Communications Corp. v. Pulse Communications Inc., 976 F. Supp. 359, 365-66 (E.D. Va. 1997) (trade secret claim contained no extra element).

f. Unfair competition claims based on the unauthorized reproduction of the plaintiff's copyrightable work are generally held to be preempted. *See, e.g.*, Kodadek v. MTV Networks, Inc., 152 F.3d 1209, 1212-13 (9th Cir. 1998); Kregos v. Associated Press, 795 F. Supp. 1325 (S.D.N.Y. 1992), *aff'd*, 3 F.3d 656 (2d Cir. 1993); Marobie-FL, Inc. v. Nat'l Ass'n of Fire Equipment Distributors, 983 F. Supp. 1167, 1180 (N.D. Ill. 1997) (unauthorized copying and distribution of clip art on web page).

g. Most courts have found that the Copyright Act preempts state law claims of conversion. *See, e.g.*, United States ex rel. Berge v. Board of Trustees of Univ. of Alabama, 104 F.3d 1453 (4th Cir. 1997); Daboub v. Gibbons, 42 F.3d 285 (5th Cir. 1995); Dielsi v. Falk, 916 F. Supp. 985 (C.D. Cal. 1996) (any claim dependent on an allegation of wrongful use or distribution of work of authorship is preempted). *But see* G.S. Rasmussen & Assoc. v. Kalitta Flying Service, 958 F.2d 896 (9th Cir. 1992) (holding that unauthorized use of FAA Supplemental Type Certificate was more than simple copying of intellectual property).

   (1) A conversion claim will not be preempted if the claim is for the physical object embodying plaintiff's work. *See* Micro Data Base Systems, Inc. v. Nellcor Puritan-Bennett, Inc., 20 F. Supp. 2d 1258, 1262-63 (N.D. Ind. 1998).

h. There exists a split of authority regarding the preemption of breach of contract claims.

   (1) The promises of the contracting parties that are necessary for the formation of a contract renders a breach of contract claim qualitatively different from a claim of copyright infringement and therefore is not preempted. Architectronics, Inc. v. Control Systems, Inc., 935 F. Supp. 425 (S.D.N.Y. 1996).

   (2) A breach of contract claim is preempted if it is based on the enforcement of rights created by copyright law, but there is no preemption if the rights sought to be enforced are rights created by the contract. American Movie Classics Co. v. Turner Entertainment Co., 922 F. Supp. 926 (S.D.N.Y. 1996).

i. Actions for unjust enrichment are generally preempted where the claim is based on the unauthorized use of copyrightable subject matter. *See, e.g.*, Systems XIX, Inc. v. Parker, 30 F. Supp. 2d 1225, 1230-31 (N.D. Cal. 1998) (recording studio's claim based on record company's release of concert recording); Curtin v. Star Editorial Inc., 2 F. Supp. 2d 670, 674-75 (E.D. Pa. 1998) (publication of photographs).

j. State protection of sound recordings fixed before February 15, 1972, will not be preempted until February 15, 2067. 17 U.S.C. § 301(c). *See* Daboub v. Gibbons, 42 F.3d 285, 288 (5th Cir. 1995).

k. Criminal statutes.

(1) Unauthorized use of property statutes are preempted where the property at issue is copyrightable subject matter used in a manner prohibited by § 106 of the Copyright Act. *See* Ohio v. Perry, 697 N.E.2d 624 (Ohio 1998) (indictment for the unauthorized uploading, downloading, and posting of computer software on a computer bulletin board was dismissed).

IX. REMEDIES.

A. Nonstatutory Monetary Damages. 17 U.S.C. § 504(b).

1. Plaintiff in a copyright infringement action is entitled to recover actual damages suffered as a result of the infringement and any of the defendant's profits that are attributable to the infringement. *See* Frank Music Corp. v. Metro-Goldwyn-Mayer, Inc., 772 F.2d 505 (9th Cir. 1985).

a. Plaintiff's actual damages.

(1) Speculative damages are not recoverable. *See* Stevens Linen Associates, Inc. v. Mastercraft Corp., 656 F.2d 11 (2d Cir. 1981).

(2) Plaintiff's lost profits cannot be based on the same sales for which defendant's profits are claimed. *See* Abeshouse v. Ultragraphics, Inc., 754 F.2d 467 (2d Cir. 1985) (improper double-counting arises "when an infringing seller has to disgorge profits on sales that a copyright holder might have made and for which he may therefore claim damages in the form of lost profits.").

(3) Punitive damages are not available in federal copyright infringement actions. Oboler v. Goldin, 714 F.2d 211 (2d Cir. 1983).

(4) Circuits are split on the issue of prejudgment interest. *Compare* Kleier Advertising, Inc. v. Premier Pontiac, Inc., 921 F.2d 1036, 1040-41 (10th Cir. 1990) (holding that prejudgment interest may indeed be awarded under the 1976 Act) *with* Robert R. Jones Assoc., Inc. v. Nino Homes, 858 F.2d 274, 282 (6th Cir.1988) (vacating an award of prejudgment interest).

b. Defendant's profits.

(1) Plaintiff is required to prove the gross revenues of the defendant's activities.

(a) Plaintiff may recover damages arising from foreign infringing uses if the predicate act of infringement occurring within the United States enabled further reproduction abroad. *See* Los Angeles News Service v. Reuters Television Int'l, Limited, 149 F.3d 987, 991-92 (9th Cir. 1998); Update Art, Inc. v. Modiin Publ'g, Ltd., 843 F.2d 67, 73 (2d Cir. 1988).

(2) Defendant is required to prove the costs incurred in generating the gross revenues as well as the allocation of costs and profits. *See* ABKCO Music, Inc. v. Harrisongs Music, Ltd., 508 F. Supp. 798 (S.D.N.Y. 1981).

B. Statutory Damages. 17 U.S.C. § 504(c).

1. The 1976 Copyright Act provides for statutory damages. The exact amount is discretionary with the jury or judge. The range of the statutory damages is a minimum of $750 and a maximum of $30,000 per infringement (all the infringements of a particular work by a particular infringer).

a. A court has wide discretion in determining the amount of statutory damages to be awarded. *See* Peer Int'l Corp. v. Pausa Records, Inc., 909 F.2d 1332, 1336 (9th Cir.

1990); Harris v. Emus Records Corp., 734 F.2d 1329, 1335 (4th Cir. 1984).

b. Among the factors a court may consider in setting statutory damage amounts are: the expenses saved and profits reaped by the infringer, the deterrent effect of the award on defendant and on third parties, and the infringer's state of mind in committing the infringement. *See* Nintendo of America, Inc. v. Dragon Pacific Int'l, 40 F.3d 1007, 1011 (9th Cir. 1994); Playboy Enterprises, Inc. v. Webbworld, Inc., 968 F. Supp. 1171, 1176 (N.D. Tex. 1997).

2. Registration with the Copyright Office at the time of the infringement is a condition precedent to obtaining statutory damages. 17 U.S.C. § 412.

   a. Where the infringement began prior to registration, but continues after registration, the plaintiff is limited to actual damages. *See* Business Trends Analysts v. Freedonia Group, Inc., 887 F.2d 339 (2d Cir. 1989).

3. The court has the discretion to reduce the minimum statutory damage to $200 in the case of innocent infringement. 17 U.S.C. § 504(c)(2).

   a. The defendant has the burden of proving that it "was not aware and had no reason to believe that [its] acts constituted an infringement of copyright." 17 U.S.C. § 504(c)(2); Los Angeles News Service v. Reuters Television Int'l, Limited, 149 F.3d 987, 995 (9th Cir. 1998).

   b. The innocent infringement reduction in statutory damages is not available where the copyrighted work contained a proper copyright notice. 17 U.S.C. §§ 401(d), 402(d).

4. The court has the discretion to increase the maximum statutory damage to $150,000 in the case of willful infringement. 17 U.S.C. § 504(c)(2).

   a. An infringement is "willful" if the actions of the defendant were taken "with knowledge that the defendant's conduct constitutes copyright infringement." Peer

Int'l Corp. v. Pausa Records, Inc., 909 F.2d 1332, 1335 n.3 (9th Cir. 1990). *See* Broadcast Music, Inc. v. Zanthas, Inc., 855 F.2d 233, 236 (5th Cir. 1988).

(1) The defendant's actual or constructive knowledge proves willfulness. Fitzgerald Publishing Co., Inc. v. Baylor Publishing Co., Inc., 807 F.2d 1110, 1115 (2d Cir. 1986); N.A.S. Import, Corp. v. Chenson Enterprises, Inc., 968 F.2d 250, 252 (2d Cir. 1992) (reckless disregard of the copyright holder's right is sufficient to warrant award of enhanced damages).

(2) Evidence of willful infringement includes defendant's ignoring plaintiff's notices about copyright protection. *See* Chi-Boy Music v. Charlie Club, Inc., 930 F.2d 1224, 1227 (7th Cir. 1991); Halnat Publ. Co. v. L.A.P.A., Inc., 669 F. Supp. 933, 937 (D. Minn. 1987).

b. A court need not find that an infringer acted maliciously to find willful infringement. *See* Fallaci v. New Gazette Literary Corp., 568 F. Supp. 1172, 1173 (S.D.N.Y. 1983).

5. The statutory damage award is inclusive of all infringements of one work by a defendant.

a. Each additional work may act as a multiplier. *See* Columbia Pictures Television v. Krypton Broadcasting, Inc., 106 F.3d 284 (9th Cir. 1997), *rev'd and remanded on other grounds*, 118 S. Ct. 1279 (1998).

(1) Each episode of a television series is a separate work for purposes of statutory damages. Columbia Pictures Television v. Krypton Broadcasting of Birmingham, Inc., 106 F.3d 284, 295 (9th Cir. 1997), *rev'd and remanded on other grounds*, 118 S. Ct. 1279 (1998); MCA Television Ltd. v. Feltner, 89 F.3d 766 (11th Cir. 1996); Twin Peaks Productions, Inc. v. Publications International, Inc., 996 F.2d 1366 (2d Cir. 1993).

b. Each separately liable infringer involved in the suit acts as a multiplier. *See* Columbia Pictures Television v. Krypton Broadcasting, Inc., 106 F.3d 284 (9th Cir. 1997), *rev'd and remanded on other grounds*, 118 S. Ct. 1279 (1998).

c. All the parts of a compilation or derivative work constitute one work for purposes of statutory damage calculations. 17 U.S.C. § 504(c)(1).

6. Under the 1976 Copyright Act it is the plaintiff's election to receive either nonstatutory or statutory damages. *See* Jordan v. Time, Inc., 111 F.3d 102 (11th Cir. 1997).

7. Recovery for statutory damages under the Copyright Act and an award for trebled profits under the Lanham Act is permitted. This is not considered a double recovery because the interests protected by the copyright law are separate from the interests protected by trademark law. Nintendo v. Dragon Pacific Int'l, 40 F.3d 1007 (9th Cir. 1994).

C. Injunctive Relief. 17 U.S.C. § 502.

1. Injunctive relief is a traditional remedy for copyright infringement. *See, e.g.*, United Feature Syndicate, Inc. v. Sunrise Mold Co., Inc., 569 F. Supp. 1475 (S.D. Fla. 1983).

a. Injunctive relief is especially favored where there is a history of continuing infringement and a substantial threat of continued infringement. *See* Walt Disney Co. v. Powell, 897 F.2d 565, 568 (D.C. Cir.1990).

2. Traditionally, when considering a motion for an injunction in a copyright infringement case, courts traditionally analyze four elements. *See* Warren Pub., Inc. v. Microdos Data Corp., 115 F.3d 1509, 1516 (11th Cir.1997).

a. Irreparable harm.

(1) The plaintiff must establish that it has an inadequate remedy at law and would suffer irreparable harm if a preliminary injunction does not issue.

(2) A presumption of irreparable injury arises if the plaintiff is able to show a likelihood of success on the merits of its copyright infringement claim. ABKCO Music, Inc. v. Stellar Records, Inc., 96 F.3d 60, 65 (2d Cir. 1996); Apple Computer, Inc. v. Formula Int'l, Inc.,

725 F.2d 521, 525-26 (9th Cir. 1984). *But see* Plains Cotton Cooperative Ass'n v. Goodpasture Computer Service, Inc., 807 F.2d 1256, 1261 (5th Cir. 1987) (Fifth Circuit does not presume irreparable harm on a showing of likelihood of success on the merits).

(a) The availability of money damages does not rebut the presumption of irreparable harm. Cadence Design Systems, Inc. v. Avanti! Corp., 125 F.3d 824 (9th Cir. 1997).

(b) Undue delay in seeking a preliminary injunction may rebut the presumption. *See* Richard Feiner and Co. v. Turner Ent. Co., 98 F.3d 33, 34 (2d Cir. 1996).

b. Success on the merits.

(1) For a preliminary injunction, a likelihood of success on the merits must be shown.

(a) The movant must show a reasonable probability of eventual success in the litigation. *See* Value Group, Inc. v. Mendham Lake Estates, L.P., 800 F. Supp. 1228, 1232 (D.N.J. 1992).

(2) For a permanent injunction, success on the merits must be proven. Sony Music Entertainment, Inc., v. Global Arts Productions, 45 F. Supp. 2d 1345, 1347 (S.D. Fla. 1999).

c. Balancing of competing claims of injury to the parties.

(1) The court must weight the irreparable harm the nonmovant will suffer if the injunction is granted against the irreparable harm to the movant if relief is denied.

d. Consideration of the public interest.

(1) The court must consider the effect granting or denying the injunction will have on nonparties. *See* Value Group, Inc. v. Mendham Lake Estates, L.P., 800 F. Supp. 1228, 1234 (D.N.J. 1992) ("The public has no interest in permitting one company to copy another company's work.").

3. In the Ninth Circuit a preliminary injunction will issue when the moving party shows (1) probable success on the merits and the possibility of irreparable harm if the injunction is not granted, or (2) serious questions as to the merits and a sharp tilt in the balance of hardships toward the moving party. Official Airlines Guides, Inc. v. Goss, 856 F.2d 85, 87 (9th Cir. 1988).

4. In the Second Circuit a preliminary injunction will issue where the moving party demonstrates a material threat of irreparable injury, and either (a) a likelihood of success on the merits, or (b) sufficiently serious questions going to the merits to make them fair grounds for litigation and a balance of hardships tipping decidedly in favor of the movant. *See* Richard Feiner and Co. v. Turner Ent. Co., 98 F.3d 33, 34 (2d Cir. 1996).

    a. To the extent that the movant seeks a mandatory injunction or substantially all of the relief to which it would be entitled were it to prevail in the action, it must show a "clear" or "substantial" likelihood of ultimate success or that it would suffer "extreme or very serious damage" absent preliminary relief. Tom Doherty Assocs., Inc. v. Saban Entertainment, Inc., 60 F.3d 27, 33-34 (2d Cir. 1995).

5. Injunctive relief may be extended to use of works to be created in the future. *See* Princeton University Press v. Michigan Document Services, Inc., 99 F.3d 1381, 1392-93 (6th Cir. 1996) (en banc); Pacific and Southern Co., Inc. v. Duncan, 744 F.2d 1490 (11th Cir.1984).

D. Impounding and Destruction of Infringing Articles. 17 U.S.C. § 503.

1. Courts have become increasingly wary of permitting *ex parte* seizure orders under the Copyright Act. *See e.g.* Paramount Pictures Corp. v. Doe, 821 F. Supp. 82, 87 (E.D.N.Y. 1993) ("a literal reading of the rules [regarding *ex parte* seizures] would result in procedures of dubious constitutional validity in light of Supreme Court decisions handed down since the time of the rules' adoption.").

E. Costs of Suit. 17 U.S.C. § 505.

1. The court has the discretion to allow the recovery of full costs by or against any party other than the United States or its officers.

2. Recoverable expenses include court fees, printing, photocopying, expert fees, and cost of interpreters. *See* Brewer-Giorgio v. Bergman, 985 F. Supp. 1478, 1485 (N.D. Ga. 1997).

F. Attorneys Fees. 17 U.S.C. § 505.

1. Registration with the Copyright Office at the time of the infringement is a condition precedent to obtaining attorneys fees. 17 U.S.C. § 412.

2. The court in its discretion may award a reasonable attorney's fee to the prevailing party. The Supreme Court has rejected any dual standard which treats prevailing plaintiffs differently than prevailing defendants under § 505. Fogerty v. Fantasy, Inc., 510 U.S. 517 (1994).

   a. Apart from exhorting courts to exercise "equitable discretion," the Court provided no clearly defined standard for courts to use in deciding whether to award attorney's fees, stating "[t]here is no precise rule or formula for making these determinations. . . ." The Court did, however, cite with approval several factors currently used by the Third Circuit. These factors include "frivolousness, motivation, objective unreasonableness (both in the factual and in the legal components of the case) and the need in particular circumstances to advance considerations of compensation and deterrence." Fogerty v. Fantasy, Inc., 510 U.S. 517, 534 n.19 (1994), *quoting*, Lieb v. Topstone Industries, Inc., 788 F.2d 151, 156 (3d Cir. 1986); Budget Cinema, Inc. v. Watertower Associates and McCloud Construction, Inc., 81 F.3d 729 (7th Cir. 1996); Historical Research Center, Inc. v. Cabral, 80 F.3d 377 (9th Cir. 1996) ("exceptional circumstances" are not a prerequisite to an award of attorney fees).

3. Attorneys fees may be awarded for legal services expended during an appeal. *See, e.g.*, Los Angeles News Service v. Reuters Television Int'l, Limited, 149 F.3d 987, 997 (9th Cir. 1998).

4. An award of attorneys fees must be reasonable. Moorish Vanguard Concert v. Brown, 498 F. Supp. 830 (E.D. Pa. 1980).

   a. The reasonableness of a particular fee award depends on a case-by-case analysis. Fantasy, Inc. v. Fogerty, 94 F.3d 553, 561 (9th Cir. 1996) (affirming an award of $1,374,519 in attorney fees to prevailing defendant).

   b. The "reasonable" fees are based on a lodestar figure represented by the reasonable hourly rate multiplied by the hours expended in the litigation. *See* Pinkham v. Camex, Inc., 84 F.3d 292 (8th Cir. 1996).

X. ENHANCED PROTECTION FOR DIGITAL MATERIALS.

A. Digital Millennium Copyright Act, signed into law by President Clinton on October 28, 1998, provides increased protection for the digital transmission and licensing of works protected by copyright.

B. Circumvention of Copyright Protection Systems. 17 U.S.C. § 1201.

1. The Act prohibits the circumvention of technological protection measures, such as scrambling or encryption, put in place by a copyright owner to control access to a copyrighted work. 17 U.S.C. § 1201(a).

   a. This prohibition takes effect two years after the enactment of the DMCA.

2. The Act prohibits the manufacture and distribution of products and services used to defeat technological measures used to control access or to protect the rights of a copyright owner, e.g. reproduction. 17 U.S.C. § 1201(a) & (b).

   a. This prohibition applies only to those devices that are primarily designed or produced for the purpose of circumventing the technological measure, or have only limited commercially significant purposes other than to circumvent the technological measure, or are marketed by persons with knowledge of their use in circumventing the technological measure.

b. This prohibition takes effect immediately.

3. Existing rights, remedies, limitations, or defenses to copyright infringement, including fair use, are not to be affected. 17 U.S.C. § 1201(c).

4. Exemption for Nonprofit Libraries, Archives and Educational Institutions. 17 U.S.C. § 1201(d).

   a. The Act creates a limited exemption permitting these institutions to gain unauthorized access to a commercially exploited copyrighted work in order to make a good faith determination of whether to acquire a copy of that work.

5. Exception for Law Enforcement, Intelligence, and Other Government Activities. 17 U.S.C. § 1201(e).

   a. Any lawfully authorized investigative, protective, information security, or intelligence activity of federal, state or local law enforcement or intelligence agencies is not prohibited by the Act.

6. Exception for Reverse Engineering. 17 U.S.C. § 1201(f).

   a. Permits circumvention of technological measures as a step in reverse engineering necessary to achieve interoperability of an independently created computer program with other programs, to the extent such reverse engineering is otherwise permitted by copyright law.

7. Exception for Encryption Research. 17 U.S.C. § 1201(g).

   a. Permits the circumvention of a technological measure in furtherance of good faith encryption research.

8. Exception Regarding Minors. 17 U.S.C. § 1201(h).

   a. Permits the manufacture of a circumvention device the sole purpose of which is to prevent the access of minors to material on the Internet.

9. Protection of Personally Identifying Information. 17 U.S.C. § 1201(i).

    a. Permits the circumvention of a technological measure that effectively controls access to a copyrighted work where the measure contains the capability of collecting or disseminating personally identifying information reflecting the online activities of a person who seeks to gain access to the copyrighted work, such as a "cookie," unless the person is given conspicuous notice and the capability to prevent or restrict the collection or dissemination of such personally identifying information.

10. Exception for Security Testing. 17 U.S.C. § 1201(j).

    a. Permits circumvention of technological measures as part of security testing, so long as the testing is otherwise permitted by law.

11. Protection of Certain Analog Devices and Certain Technological Measures. 17 U.S.C. § 1201(k).

    a. Prohibits the circumvention of two current forms of analog copy control technology, automatic gain control and colorstripe copy control, by redesigned video recorders or "black box" devices. The Act requires analog video cassette recorders to conform to these forms of copy control technology.

    b. Professional analog video cassette recorders are exempted.

    c. This provision takes effect 18 months after the enactment of the DMCA.

C. Integrity of Copyright Management Information (CMI). 17 U.S.C. § 1202.

1. "Copyright Management Information" includes information that identifies a copyrighted work, its author, its copyright owner, its creator, as well as terms and conditions for use of the work. 17 U.S.C. § 1202(c)

2. The Act prohibits the providing or distribution of false copyright management information, 17 U.S.C. § 1202(a), and the removal or alteration of CMI, 17 U.S.C. § 1202(b).

3. Exception for Law Enforcement, Intelligence, and Other Government Activities. 17 U.S.C. § 1202(d).

    a. Any lawfully authorized investigative, protective, information security, or intelligence activity of federal, state or local law enforcement or intelligence agencies is not prohibited by the Act.

4. Limitations on Liability. 17 U.S.C. § 1202(e).

    a. Analog Transmissions.

        (1) A broadcast station, cable system or program provider will not be liable for violating the CMI requirements if:

            (a) avoiding the violation is not technically feasible or would create an undue financial hardship; and

            (b) there was no intent to infringe a copyright.

    b. Digital Transmissions.

        (1) Until a digital transmission standard for the placement of CMI is set in a voluntary, consensus standard-setting process, a broadcast station, cable system or program provider will not be liable for violating the CMI requirements if:

            (a) there was no intent to infringe a copyright, and

                i) the transmission of CMI would result in a perceptible visual or aural degradation of the digital signal, or

                ii) the transmission of CMI would conflict with an applicable government regulation or industry-wide standard.

D. Civil Remedies. 17 U.S.C. § 1203.

1. For violations of sections 1201 and 1202, the federal district court has broad remedial powers.

    a. Injunctions.

    b. Impoundment.

c. Damages.

(1) Actual damages.

(a) Actual damages suffered by the plaintiff.

(b) Defendant's profits.

(2) Statutory damages.

(a) For each violation of § 1201, $200-2,500 per act of circumvention.

(b) For each violation of § 1202, $2,500-25,000 for each violation.

(3) Repeated violations.

(a) For any repeated violation within three years, the court may increase the award of damages up to triple the amount that would otherwise be awarded.

(4) Innocent violations.

(a) The court may reduce or remit the total award of damages where the violator was not aware and had no reason to believe that its acts constituted a violation.

d. Recovery of costs.

e. Reasonable attorney's fees.

f. Order the remedial modification or the destruction of any device or product involved in the violation.

E. Criminal penalties. 17 U.S.C. § 1204.

1. For willful violations of sections 1201 and 1202 for purposes of commercial advantage or private financial gain, the defendant can be fined:

a. for the first offense, up to $500,000 and imprisoned for up to five years or both.

b. for subsequent offenses, up to $1,000,000 and imprisoned for up to ten years or both.

2. 5 year statute of limitations.
3. Criminal penalties do not apply to nonprofit libraries, archives or educational institutions.

Appendix A

Table of Cases

Abeshouse v. Ultragraphics, Inc., 754 F.2d 467 (2d Cir. 1985) 145

ABKCO Music, Inc. v. Harrisongs Music, Ltd., 508 F. Supp. 798 (S.D.N.Y. 1981) 146

ABKCO Music, Inc. v. Stellar Records, Inc., 96 F.3d 60 (2d Cir. 1996) 2, 65, 149

ABKCO Music, Inc. v. Westminster Music, Ltd. 838 F. Supp. 153 (S.D.N.Y. 1993), *aff'd*, 41 F.3d 1502 (2d Cir. 1994) 58

Academy of Motion Picture Arts and Sciences v. Creative House Promotions, Inc., 944 F.2d 1446 (9th Cir. 1991) 81

Acuff-Rose Music, Inc. v. Josten's, Inc., 155 F.3d 140 (2d Cir. 1998) 6

Addison-Wesley Publishing Co., Inc. v. New York University, 1983 Copyright L. Dec. (CCH) ¶25,544 (S.D.N.Y. 1983) 136

Adsani v. Miller, 139 F.3d 67 (2d Cir. 1998) 104

Advanced Computer Services of Michigan v. MAI Systems, Corp., 845 F. Supp. 356 (E.D. Va. 1994) 3, 64

Agee v. Paramount Communications, Inc., 59 F.3d 317 (2d Cir. 1995) 64, 68

Ahn v. Midway Mfging Co., 965 F. Supp. 1134 (N.D. Ill. 1997) 143

Alberto-Culver Co. v. Andrea Dumon, Inc., 466 F.2d 705 (7th Cir. 1972) 6

Alcatel USA, Inc. v. DGI Technologies, Inc., 166 F.3d 772 (5th Cir. 1999) 140, 143

Alexander v. Haley, 460 F. Supp. 40 (S.D.N.Y. 1978) 15

Alfred Bell & Co. v. Catalda Fine Arts, Inc., 191 F.2d 99 (2d Cir. 1951) 5, 7

Aliotti v. Dakin & Co., 831 F.2d 898 (9th Cir. 1987). 107

All Nations Music v. Christian Family Network, Inc., 989 F. Supp. 863 (W.D. Mich. 1997) 112

Allarcom Pay Television Ltd. v. General Instrument Corp., 69 F.3d 381 (9th Cir. 1995) 142

Allen v. Academic Games League of America, Inc., 89 F.3d 614 (9th Cir. 1996). 70

Allen-Myland, Inc. v. Int'l Business Machines Corp., 746 F. Supp. 520, 536 (E.D. Pa. 1990) 24

Almo Music Corp. v. 77 East Adam, Inc., 647 F. Supp. 123 (N.D. Ill. 1986) 110

Alva Studios, Inc. v. Winniger, 177 F. Supp. 265 (S.D.N.Y. 1959). 34

American Dental Ass'n v. Delta Dental Plans Ass'n, 126 F.3d 977 (7th Cir. 1997) 9, 10

American Geophysical Union v. Texaco, Inc., 37 F.3d 881 (2d Cir. 1994) 121

American Movie Classics Co. v. Turner Entertainment Co., 922 F. Supp. 926 (S.D.N.Y. 1996). 144

American Tobacco Co. v. Werckmeister, 207 U.S. 284 (1907) 82

American Vitagraph, Inc. v. Levy, 659 F.2d 1023 (9th Cir. 1981). 81

Amsterdam v. Triangle Publications, 93 F. Supp. 79 (E.D. Pa. 1950), *aff'd on opinion below*, 189 F.2d 104 (3d Cir. 1951) 26

Apple Computer, Inc. v. Formula Int'l, Inc., 725 F.2d 521 (9th Cir. 1984) 149

Apple Computer, Inc. v. Franklin Computer Corp., 714 F.2d 1240 (3d Cir. 1983) 19, 20

Apple Computer, Inc. v. Microsoft Corp., 35 F.3d 1435 (9th Cir. 1994) 22, 30, 38

Architectronics, Inc. v. Control Systems, Inc., 935 F. Supp. 425 (S.D.N.Y. 1996). 144

Armento v. Laser Image, Inc., 950 F. Supp. 719 (W.D.N.C. 1996) 47
Arnstein v. Porter, 154 F.2d 464 (2d Cir. 1946) 109
Arthur Rutenberg Homes, Inc. v. Drew Homes, Inc., 29 F.3d 1529 (11th Cir. 1994) 53
Artists Music, Inc. v. Reed Publishing, Inc., 31 U.S.P.Q. 2d 1623 (S.D.N.Y. 1994) 112
Association of American Medical Colleges v. Mikaelian, 571 F. Supp. 144 (E.D. Pa.), *aff'd*, 734 F.2d 3 (3d Cir. 1983) 123
Atari Games Corp. v. Oman, 888 F.2d 878 (D.C. Cir. 1989) 6, 39
Atari Games Corp. v. Nintendo of America, Inc., 975 F.2d 832 (Fed. Cir. 1992) 21, 30
Autoskill, Inc. v. National Educational Support Systems, Inc., 994 F.2d 1476 (10th Cir. 1993) 43
Avtec Systems, Inc. v. Peiffer, 21 F.3d 568 (4th Cir. 1994) 45
Aymes v. Bonelli, 47 F.3d 23 (2d Cir. 1995) 25, 43
Baker v. Selden, 101 U.S. 99 (1879) 9, 11
Bagdadi v. Nazar, 84 F.3d 1194 (9th Cir. 1996) 83
Bailie v. Fisher, 258 F.2d 425 (D.C. Cir. 1958) 6
Ballas v. Tedesco, 41 F. Supp. 2d 531 (D.N.J. 1999) 53
Baltimore Orioles, Inc. v. Major League Baseball Players Ass'n, 805 F.2d 663 (7th Cir. 1986) 143
Bartsch v. Metro-Goldwyn Mayer, Inc., 391 F.2d 150, 155 (2d Cir.1968) 57
Batjac Productions Inc. v. Goodtimes Home Video Corp., 160 F.3d 1223 (9th Cir. 1998) 81
Bellsouth Advertising & Publishing Corporation v. Donnelly Information Publishing, Inc., 933 F.2d 952 (11th Cir. 1991) 37
Benny v. Loew's, Inc., 239 F.2d 532 (9th Cir. 1956), *aff'd by an equally divided court*, 356 U.S. 43 (1958) 128
Berlin v. E.C. Publications, 329 F.2d 541 (2d Cir. 1964) 134, 135
Bibbero Systems, Inc. v. Colwell Systems, Inc., 893 F.2d 1104 (9th Cir. 1990) 11

Bleistein v. Donaldson Lithographing Co., 188 U.S. 239 (1903) 7

Boosey & Hawkes Music Publishers, Ltd. v. Walt Disney Co., 145 F.3d 481 (2d Cir. 1998) 58

Botello v. Shell Oil Co., 229 Cal. App. 3d 1130, 280 Cal. Rptr. 535 (1991). 79

Bourne v. Walt Disney Co., 68 F.3d 621 (2d Cir. 1995) 137

BPI Systems, Inc. v. Leith, 532 F. Supp. 208 (W.D. Tex. 1981) 46

Brandir International, Inc. v. Cascade Pacific Lumber Co. , 834 F.2d 1142 (2d Cir. 1987) 26, 28

Brewer-Giorgio v. Bergman, 985 F. Supp. 1478 (N.D. Ga. 1997) 152

Bridgeman Art Library, Ltd. v. Corel Corp., 36 F. Supp. 2d 191 (S.D.N.Y. 1999) 8, 9

Bright Tunes Music Corp. v. Harrisongs Music, Ltd., 420 F. Supp. 177 (S.D.N.Y. 1976), *aff'd sub nom.* ABKCO Music, Inc. v. Harrisongs Music, Ltd., 722 F.2d 988 (2d Cir. 1983) 106, 110

Broadcast Music, Inc. v. Claire's Boutiques, Inc., 949 F.2d 1482 (7th Cir. 1991) 72

Broadcast Music, Inc. v. Hirsch, 104 F.3d 1163 (9th Cir. 1997). 57

Broadcast Music, Inc. v. Zanthas, Inc., 855 F.2d 233 (5th Cir. 1988) 148

Brown Instrument Co. v. Warner, 161 F.2d 910 (D.C. Cir. 1947) 11

BTE v. Bonnecaze, 43 F. Supp. 2d 619 (E.D. La. 1999) 49, 51

Buchwald v. Paramount Pictures Corp., 13 U.S.P.Q.2d 1497 (Cal. Sup. Ct. 1990) 12

Buck v. Jewell-La Salle Realty Co., 283 U.S. 191 (1931) 70

Budget Cinema, Inc. v. Watertower Associates and McCloud Construction, Inc., 81 F.3d 729 (7th Cir. 1996). 152

Building Officials & Code Administrators International v. Code Technology, Inc., 628 F.2d 730 (1st Cir. 1980) 40

Burke v. National Broadcasting Co., 598 F.2d 688 (1st Cir.) 80, 81

Burroughs v. Metro-Goldwyn-Mayer, Inc., 683 F.2d 610 (2d Cir. 1982) 96

Burrow-Giles Lithographic Co. v. Sarony, 111 U.S. 53 (1884) 7

Burwood Co. v. Marsel Mirror & Glass Products, Inc., 468 F. Supp. 1215 (N.D. Ill. 1979) 68, 75

Business Trends Analysts v. Freedonia Group, Inc., 887 F.2d 339 (2d Cir. 1989). 147

C.M. Paula Co. v. Logan, 355 F. Supp. 189 (N.D. Tex. 1973) 68

Cadence Design Systems, Inc. v. Avanti! Corp., 125 F.3d 824 (9th Cir. 1997) 150

Campbell v. Acuff-Rose Music, Inc., 510 U.S. 569 (1994). 7, 118–121, 123–125, 127–130, 132–134

Carol Barnhart, Inc. v. Economy Cover Corp., 773 F.2d 411 (2d Cir. 1985) 28

Carter v. Helmsley-Spear, Inc., 71 F.3d 77 (2d Cir. 1995) 76

Castle Rock Entertainment, Inc. v. Carol Publishing Group, Inc., 150 F.3d 132 (2d Cir. 1998) 120, 130

CCC Information Services, Inc. v. MacLean Hunter Market Reports, Inc., 44 F.3d 61 (2d Cir. 1994) 40

Central Point Software, Inc. v. Global Software & Accessories, Inc., 880 F. Supp. 957 (S.D.N.Y. 1995) 69

Charles Garnier, Paris v. Andin Int'l, Inc., 36 F.3d 1214 (1st Cir. 1994) 84

Chase-Riboud v. Dreamworks, Inc., 987 F. Supp. 1222 (C.D. Cal. 1997) 17

Chavez v. Arte Publico Press, 139 F.3d 504 (5th Cir. 1998) 104

Childress v. Taylor, 945 F.2d 500 (2d Cir. 1991) 49, 50

Chi-Boy Music v. Charlie Club, Inc., 930 F.2d 1224 (7th Cir. 1991) 148

City Consumer Services, Inc. v. Horne, 100 F.R.D. 740 (D. Utah 1983) 14

Classic Film Museum, Inc. v. Warner Bros., Inc., 453 F. Supp. 852 (D. Me. 1978), *aff'd*, 597 F.2d 13 (1st Cir. 1979) 81

Clevenger v. Baker, Voorhis & Co., 8 N.Y.2d 187, 168 N.E.2d 643 (1960) 79

Cohen v. Paramount Pictures Corp., 845 F.2d 851 (9th Cir. 1988) 58, 59

Columbia Pictures Industries, Inc. v. Aveco, Inc., 800 F.2d 59 (3d Cir. 1986) 71

Columbia Pictures Industries, Inc. v. Miramax Films Corp., 11 F. Supp. 2d 1179 (C.D. Cal. 1998) 133, 135

Columbia Pictures Industries, Inc. v. Professional Real Estate Investors, Inc., 866 F.2d 278 (9th Cir. 1989) 71

Columbia Pictures Industries, Inc. v. Redd Horne, Inc., 749 F.2d 154 (3d Cir. 1984) 71

Columbia Pictures Television v. Krypton Broadcasting, Inc., 106 F.3d 284 (9th Cir. 1997), *rev'd and remanded on other grounds*, 118 S. Ct. 1279 (1998) 110, 148

Community For Creative Non-Violence v. Reid, 490 U.S. 730 (1989) 2, 41, 43

Computer Associates International, Inc. v. Altai, Inc., 982 F.2d 693 (2d Cir. 1992) 21, 22, 107

Consumers Union of United States, Inc. v. General Signal Corp., 724 F.2d 1044 (2d Cir. 1983) 125

Corcovado Music Corp. v. Hollis Music, Inc., 981 F.2d 679 (2d Cir. 1993) 55

Cortner v. Israel, 732 F.2d 267 (2d Cir. 1984) 101

Craft v. Kobler, 667 F. Supp. 120 (S.D.N.Y. 1987) 126

Crimi v. Rutgers Presbyterian Church, 194 Misc. 570, 89 N.Y.S.2d 813 (Sup. Ct. 1949) 76

Curb v. MCA Records, Inc., 898 F. Supp. 586 (M.D. Tenn. 1995) 63

Curtin v. Star Editorial Inc., 2 F. Supp. 2d 670 (E.D. Pa. 1998) 9, 144

Daboub v. Gibbons, 42 F.3d 285 (5th Cir. 1995) 139, 142, 144, 145

Dallas Cowboys Cheerleaders, Inc. v. Scoreboard Posters, Inc., 600 F.2d 1184 (5th Cir. 1979) 138

Danjaq, S.A. v. MGM/UA Communications Co., 773 F. Supp. 194 (C.D. Cal. 1991) 63

Data Cash Sys., Inc. v. JS&A Group, Inc., 628 F.2d 1039 (7th Cir. 1980) 80

Davies v. Bowes, 209 F. 53 (S.D.N.Y. 1913) 17

Desny v. Wilder, 46 Cal. 2d 715, 299 P.2d 257 (1956) 12

Dielsi v. Falk, 916 F. Supp. 985 (C.D. Cal. 1996) 144

Devils Films, Inc. v. Nectar Video, 29 F. Supp. 2d 174 (S.D.N.Y. 1998) 141

Digital Communication Associates, Inc. v. Softklone Distributing Corp., 659 F. Supp. 449 (N.D. Ga. 1987) 22

Dolman v. Agee, 157 F.3d 708 (9th Cir. 1998) 41, 42, 80

Donna v. Dodd, Mead & Co., Inc., 374 F. Supp. 429 (S.D.N.Y. 1974) 52

Dr. Seuss Enterprises, L.P. v. Penguin Books USA, Inc., 109 F.3d 1394 (9th Cir. 1997) 133

DSC Communications Corp. v. Pulse Communications, Inc., 170 F.3d 1354 (Fed. Cir. 1999) 24, 111, 143

Duffy v. Penguin Books USA Inc., 4 F. Supp. 2d 268 (S.D.N.Y. 1998) 126

Easter Seal Society for Crippled Children and Adults of Louisiana, Inc. v. Playboy Enterprises, 815 F.2d 324 (5th Cir. 1987) 42

Eckes v. Card Prices Update, 736 F.2d 859 (2d Cir. 1984) 36

Eden Toys, Inc. v. Florelee Undergarment Co., 697 F.2d 27 (2d Cir. 1982) 53

Edison Brothers Stores, Inc. v. Broadcast Music, Inc., 954 F.2d 1419 (8th Cir. 1992) 72

Edward B. Marks Music Corp. v. Jerry Vogel Music Co., 140 F.2d 266 (2d Cir. 1944) 49

Effects Associates, Inc. v. Cohen, 908 F.2d 555 (1990) 48, 53, 54

Elsmere Music, Inc. v. National Broadcasting Co., 482 F. Supp. 741 (S.D.N.Y.), *aff'd*, 623 F.2d 252, 253 (2d Cir. 1980) 129, 134

EMSA Limited Partnership v. Lincoln, 691 So. 2d 547 (Fla. Ct. App. 1997) 102

Encyclopedia Britannica Educational Corp. v. Crooks, 447 F. Supp. 243 (W.D.N.Y. 1978) 124, 128

Engineering Dynamics, Inc. v. Structural Software, Inc., 26 F.3d 1335 (5th Cir. 1994) 22

Entertainment Research Group, Inc. v. Genesis Creative Group, Inc., 122 F.3d 1211 (9th Cir. 1997) 7, 9, 34

Erickson v. Trinity Theatre, Inc., 13 F.3d 1061 (7th Cir. 1994) 50

Esquire v. Ringer, 591 F.2d 796 (D.C. Cir. 1979) 26

Estate of Hemingway v. Random House, Inc., 23 N.Y.2d 341, 296 N.Y.S.2d 771, 244 N.E.2d 250 (1969) 15

Estate of Martin Luther King, Jr., Inc. v. CBS, Inc., 194 F.3d 1211 (2d Cir. 1999) 81

Evans and Assocs. Inc. v. Continental Homes, Inc., 785 F.2d 897 (11th Cir. 1986). 86, 105

Eve of Milady v. Impression Bridal, Inc., 957 F. Supp. 484 (S.D.N.Y. 1997) 27

Fallaci v. New Gazette Literary Corp., 568 F. Supp. 1172 (S.D.N.Y. 1983) 148

Falwell v. Penthouse International, Ltd., 521 F. Supp. 1204 (W.D. Va. 1981) 16

Fantasy, Inc. v. Fogerty, 94 F.3d 553 (9th Cir. 1996) 153

Faris v. Enberg, 97 Cal. App. 3d 309, 158 Cal. Rptr. 704 (1979) 13

Feist Publications, Inc. v. Rural Telephone Service Company, Inc., 499 U.S. 340 (1991) 5, 6, 14, 16–18, 36–38

Feltner v. Columbia Pictures Television, Inc., 118 S. Ct. 1279 (1998) 104

Filmvideo Releasing Corp. v. Hastings, 509 F. Supp. 60 (S.D.N.Y. 1981), *aff'd*, 668 F.2d 91 (2d Cir. 1981) 18

Fisher v. Dees, 794 F.2d 432 (9th Cir. 1986) 124, 125, 132, 134

Fitzgerald Publishing Co., Inc. v. Baylor Publishing Co., Inc., 807 F.2d 1110 (2d Cir. 1986) 148

Fleet v. CBS, Inc., 50 Cal. App. 4th 1911 (1996) 143

Florists' Transworld Delivery Association v. Reliable Glassware & Pottery Co., Inc., 213 U.S.P.Q. 808 (N.D. Ill. 1981) 82

Foamation, Inc. v. Wedeward Enterprises, Inc., 970 F. Supp. 676 (E.D. Wis. 1997) 83

Fogerty v. Fantasy, Inc., 510 U.S. 517 (1994) 152

Folsom v. Marsh, 9 F. Cas. 342 (1841) 118

Fonovisa, Inc. v. Cherry Auction, Inc., 76 F.3d 259 (9th Cir. 1996) 111, 112

Food Lion, Inc. v. Capital Cities/ABC, Inc., 946 F. Supp. 420 (M.D. N.C. 1996), *aff'd*, 116 F.3d 472 (4th Cir, 1997) 45

Frank Music Corp. v. Metro-Goldwyn-Mayer, Inc., 772 F.2d 505 (9th Cir. 1985) 25, 145

Franklin Mint Corp. v. National Wildlife Art Exchange, Inc., 575 F.2d 62 (3d Cir.) 11

Franklin v. Cannon Films, Inc., 654 F. Supp. 133 (C.D. Cal. 1987) 102

Fred Ahlert Music Corp. v. Warner/Chappell Music, Inc., 155 F.3d 17 (2d Cir. 1998) 97

Friedman v. Stacey Data Processing Servs., Inc., 17 U.S.P.Q.2d 1858 (N.D. Ill. 1990) 56

G. Ricordi & Co. v. Paramount Pictures, Inc., 189 F.2d 469 (2d Cir.) 34

G.S. Rasmussen & Assoc. v. Kalitta Flying Service, 958 F.2d 896 (9th Cir. 1992) 144

Gamma Audio & Video, Inc. v. Ean-Chea, 11 F.3d 1106 (1st Cir. 1993) 52, 101

Gaste v. Kaiserman, 863 F.2d 1061 (2d Cir. 1988) 106

Gates Rubber Co. v. Bando Chemical Indus., Ltd., 9 F.3d 823 (10th Cir. 1993) 21, 22, 143

Gay Toys, Inc. v. Buddy L. Corporation, 703 F.2d 970 (6th Cir. 1983). 29

GB Marketing USA, Inc. v. Gerolsteiner Brunnen GmbH & Co., 782 F. Supp. 763 (W.D.N.Y. 1991) 63

Georgia v. Harrison Co., 548 F. Supp. 110 (N.D. Ga. 1982), *vacated by agreement between the parties*, 559 F. Supp. 37 (N.D. Ga. 1983) 40

Gershwin Publishing Corp. v. Columbia Artists Management, Inc., 443 F.2d 1159 (1971). 111

Gilliam v. American Broadcasting Companies, Inc., 538 F.2d 14 (2d Cir. 1976) 76, 79

Gracen v. Bradford Exchange, 698 F.2d 300 (7th Cir. 1983). 7, 54

Graham v. James, 144 F.3d 229 (2d Cir. 1998) 76, 137

Granz v. Harris, 198 F.2d 585 (2d Cir. 1952) 79

Grove Press, Inc. v. Greenleaf Publishing Co., 247 F. Supp. 518 (E.D.N.Y. 1965) 67

Grubb v. KMS Patriots, L.P., 88 F.3d 1 (1st Cir. 1996) 5

Grundberg v. Upjohn Company, 137 F.R.D. 372, 19 U.S.P.Q.2d 1590 (D. Utah 1991) 13

Halnat Publ. Co. v. L.A.P.A., Inc., 669 F. Supp. 933 (D. Minn. 1987) 148

Harcourt, Brace & World, Inc. v. Graphic Controls Corp., 329 F. Supp. 517 (S.D.N.Y. 1971) 11

Harris v. Emus Records Corp., 734 F.2d 1329 (4th Cir. 1984). 147

Harper & Row, Publishers, Inc. v. Nation Enterprises, 471 U.S. 539 (1985). 118, 119, 122, 124–129, 131, 138

Hasbro Bradley, Inc. v. Sparkle Toys, Inc., 780 F.2d 189 (2d Cir. 1985) 82

Heim v. Universal Pictures Co., Inc., 154 F.2d 480 (2d Cir. 1946) 81

Herbert Rosenthal Jewelry Corp. v. Kalpakian, 446 F.2d 738 (9th Cir. 1971). 10

Higgins v. Detroit Education Television Foundation, 4 F. Supp. 2d 701 (E.D. Mich. 1998) 123, 127

Historical Research Center, Inc. v. Cabral, 80 F.3d 377 (9th Cir. 1996)................................ 152

Hoehling v. Universal City Studios, Inc., 618 F.2d 972 (2d Cir.).. 17

Horgan v. Macmillan, Inc., 789 F.2d 158 (2d Cir. 1986) 26

Hoste v. Radio Corp. of America, 654 F.2d 11 (6th Cir. 1981).. 139

Hotaling v. Church of Jesus Christ of Latter-Day Saints, 118 F.3d 199 (4th Cir. 1997) 68

Hubco Data Products Corp. v. Management Assistance, Inc., 219 U.S.P.Q. 450 (D. Idaho 1983).. 23

Hunt v. Pasternack, 192 F.3d 877 (9th Cir. 1999).................... 33

Hustler Magazine v. Falwell, 485 U.S. 46 (1988) 132

Hustler Magazine v. Moral Majority, Inc., 606 F. Supp. 1526 (C.D. Cal. 1985), *aff'd*, 796 F.2d 1148 (9th Cir. 1986) 123, 131

Hustler Magazine, Inc. v. Moral Majority, Inc., 796 F.2d 1148 (9th Cir. 1986) 128

I.A.E., Inc. v. Shaver, 74 F.3d 768 (7th Cir. 1996)............... 54, 137

In re AEG Acquisition Corp., 127 B.R. 34 (C.D. Cal. 1991), *aff'd*, 161 B.R. 50 (9th Cir. 1993).. 57

In re Marriage of Worth, 195 Cal. App. 3d 768, 241 Cal. Rptr. 135 (1987)............................... 52

Infinity Broadcasting Corp. v. Kirkwood, 150 F.3d 104 (2d Cir. 1998) 39, 121

In re Peregrine Entertainment Ltd., 116 B.R. 194 (C.D. Cal. 1990) 57

Iowa State University Research Foundation, Inc. v. American Broadcasting Companies, Inc., 621 F.2d 57 (2d Cir. 1980) 123

Iza Music Corp. v. W & K Music Corp., 995 F. Supp. 417 (S.D.N.Y. 1998).......................... 103

J.A. Richards, Inc. v. New York Post, Inc., 23 F. Supp. 619 (S.D.N.Y. 1938)............................ 82

Jackson v. Axton, 25 F.3d 884 (9th Cir. 1994). 140
Jackson v. MPI Home Video, 694 F. Supp. 483 (N.D. Ill. 1988) 14, 15
Jackson v. Warner Bros., Inc., 993 F. Supp. 585 (E.D. Mich. 1997) 135
Jartech, Inc. v. Clancy, 666 F.2d 403 (9th Cir. 1982) 121, 125, 141
Jarvis v. A & M Records, 827 F. Supp. 282 (D.N.J. 1993) 8, 107
Jason v. Fonda, 698 F.2d 966 (9th Cir. 1983) 105
Jeweler's Circular Publishing Co. v. Keystone Publishing Co., 274 F. 932 (S.D.N.Y. 1921), *aff'd*, 281 F. 83 (2d Cir.) 8
John Muller & Co. v. New York Arrows Soccer Team, 802 F.2d 989 (8th Cir. 1986) 6
Johnson Controls, Inc. v. Phoenix Control Systems, Inc., 886 F.2d 1173 (9th Cir. 1989) 20
Johnson v. Jones, 149 F.3d 494 (6th Cir. 1998). 54
Jordan v. Time, Inc., 111 F.3d 102 (11th Cir. 1997) 149
Kanakos v. Mx Trading Corp., 216 U.S.P.Q. 1030 (S.D.N.Y. 1981). 138
Keep Thompson Governor Committee v. Citizens for Gallen, 457 F. Supp. 957 (D.N.H. 1978) 130
Kepner-Tregoe, Inc. v. Leadership Software, Inc., 29 U.S.P.Q.2d 1747 (5th Cir. 1994). 20, 21
Kern River Gas Transmission Co. v. Coastal Corp., 899 F.2d 1458 (5th Cir.) 10
Key Publications, Inc. v. Chinatown Today Publishing Enterprises, Inc., 945 F.2d 509 (2d Cir. 1991) 37
Khandji v. Keystone Resorts Management, Inc., 140 F.R.D. 697, 23 U.S.P.Q.2d 1156 (D. Colo. 1992) 14
Kieselstein-Cord v. Accessories By Pearl, Inc., 632 F.2d 989 (2d Cir. 1980) 29
Kleier Advertising, Inc. v. Premier Pontiac, Inc., 921 F.2d 1036 (10th Cir. 1990) 146
Kodadek v. MTV Networks, Inc., 152 F.3d 1209 (9th Cir. 1998) 85, 143

Korman v. HBC Florida, Inc., 182 F.3d 1291 (11th Cir. 1999) 93, 95

Kregos v. Associated Press, 795 F. Supp. 1325 (S.D.N.Y. 1992), *aff'd*, 3 F.3d 656 (2d Cir. 1993) 143

Kregos v. Associated Press, 937 F.2d 700 (2d Cir. 1991). 10, 11, 35

Kulik Photography v. Cochran, 975 F. Supp. 812 (E.D. Va. 1997) 135

L. Batlin & Son, Inc. v. Snyder, 536 F.2d 486 (2d Cir. 1976) 9, 34

La Cienega Music Co. v. ZZ Top, 3 F.3d 950 (9th Cir. 1995). 80, 84

Lamb v. Starks, 949 F. Supp. 753 (N.D. Cal. 1996) 34

Lasercomb America, Inc. v. Reynolds, 911 F.2d 970 (4th Cir. 1990) 140

Lee v. A.R.T. Co., 125 F.3d 580 (7th Cir. 1997) 67

Leibovitz v. Paramount Pictures Corp., 137 F.3d 109 (2d Cir. 1998) 122, 133

Leicester v. Warner Bros., 47 U.S.P.Q.2d 1501 (C.D. Cal. 1998) 32, 138

Letter Edged in Black Press, Inc. v. Public Bldg. Comm'n of Chicago, 320 F. Supp. 1303 (N.D. Ill. 1970) 82

Lewis Galoob Toys, Inc. v. Nintendo of America, Inc., 964 F.2d 965 (9th Cir. 1992). 34

Lieb v. Topstone Industries, Inc., 788 F.2d 151 (3d Cir. 1986) 152

Lombardi v. Suares, 923 F. Supp. 51 (S.D.N.Y. 1996). 102

Lone Wolf McQuade Associates v. CBS, Inc., 961 F. Supp. 587 (S.D.N.Y. 1997) 18, 39, 138

Los Angeles News Service v. KCAL-TV Channel 9, 108 F.3d 1119 (9th Cir. 1997) 120, 124, 129

Los Angeles News Service v. Reuters Television Int'l, Limited, 149 F.3d 987 (9th Cir. 1998). 63, 120, 122, 127, 130, 146, 147, 153

Los Angeles News Service v. Tullo, 973 F.2d 791 (9th Cir. 1992). 8, 122

Lotus Development Corp. v. Borland International, Inc., 49 F.3d 807 (1st Cir. 1995), *aff'd by an equally divided Court*, 516 U.S. 233 (1996) 10, 23

Lulirama Ltd, Inc. v. Axcess Broadcast Services, Inc., 128 F.3d 872 (5th Cir. 1997). 44, 48, 54

MacLean Assocs., Inc. v. Wm. M. Mercer-Meidinger-Hansen, Inc., 952 F.2d 769 (3d Cir. 1991) 44

Magnuson v. Video Yesteryear, 85 F.3d 1424 (9th Cir. 1996). 47, 53

MAI Systems Corp. v. Peak Computer, Inc., 991 F.2d 511 (9th Cir. 1993) 3, 24, 64

Maljack Productions, Inc. v. Goodtimes Home Video Corp., 81 F.3d 881 (9th Cir. 1996) 30, 58

Maljack Productions, Inc. v. UAV Corp., 964 F. Supp. 1416 (C.D. Cal. 1997), *aff'd*, 160 F.3d 1223 (9th Cir. 1998). 7

Marco v. Accent Publishing Co., 969 F.2d 1547 (3d Cir. 1992) 44

Marcus v. Rowley, 695 F.2d 1171 (9th Cir. 1983) 119, 125, 127, 136

Marling v. Ellison, 218 U.S.P.Q. 702 (S.D.N.Y. 1982). 34

Marobie-FL, Inc. v. Nat'l Ass'n of Fire Equipment Distributors, 983 F. Supp. 1167 (N.D. Ill. 1997) 105, 143

Marshall v. New Kids on the Block, 780 F. Supp. 1005 (S.D.N.Y. 1991). 138

Martin Luther King, Jr. Center for Social Change Inc. v. American Heritage Products, Inc., 508 F. Supp. 854 (N.D. Ga. 1981) 122

Martin v. City of Indianapolis, 4 F. Supp. 2d 808, 809 (S.D. Ind. 1998) 79

Marvin Worth Productions v. Superior Films Corp., 319 F. Supp. 1269 (S.D.N.Y. 1970). 16

Mason v. Montgomery Data, Inc., 967 F.2d 135 (5th Cir. 1992). 26

Masquerade Novelty, Inc. v. Unique Industries, Inc., 912 F.2d 663 (3d Cir. 1990) 29
Matthew Bender & Co., Inc. v. West Publishing Co., 158 F.3d 674 (2d Cir. 1998) 36–39
Maxtone-Graham v. Burtchaell, 803 F.2d 1253 (2d Cir. 1986) 126, 127
Maxwell v. Veeck, 110 F.3d 749 (11th Cir. 1997). 54
Mayer v. Josiah Wedgwood & Sons, Ltd., 601 F. Supp. 1523 (S.D.N.Y. 1985). 141
Mazer v. Stein, 347 U.S. 201 (1954) 1, 27
MCA Television Ltd. v. Feltner, 89 F.3d 766 (11th Cir. 1996). 148
MCA, Inc. v. Wilson, 677 F.2d 180 (2d Cir. 1981) 124, 133
Meeropol v. Nizer, 560 F.2d 1061 (2d Cir. 1977) 128, 129, 131
Merchant v. Levy, 92 F.3d 51 (2d Cir. 1996) 102
Metro-Goldwyn-Mayer, Inc. v. American Honda Motor Co., Inc., 900 F. Supp. 1287 (C.D. Cal. 1995) 19, 39
Micro Data Base Systems, Inc. v. Nellcor Puritan-Bennett, Inc., 20 F. Supp. 2d 1258 (N.D. Ind. 1998) 144
Micro Star v. Formgen, Inc., 154 F.3d 1107 (9th Cir. 1998) 54, 140
Mid America Title Co. v. Kirk, 59 F.3d 719 (7th Cir. 1995). 37
Midas Productions, Inc. v. Baer, 437 F. Supp. 1388 (C.D. Cal. 1977) 14, 15, 18
Midway Mfg. Co. v. Strohon, 564 F. Supp. 741 (N.D. Ill. 1983) 25
Midway Manufacturing Co. v. Arctic International, Inc., 547 F. Supp. 999 (N.D. Ill.), *aff'd*, 704 F.2d 1009 (7th Cir. 1982). 3
Midway Manufacturing Co. v. Arctic International, Inc., 704 F.2d 1009 (7th Cir. 1982) 30
Miller v. CP Chemicals, Inc., 808 F. Supp. 1238 (D.S.C. 1992). 45

Miller v. Universal City Studios, 650 F.2d 1365 (5th Cir. 1981). 14, 17

Mills Music, Inc. v. Arizona, 187 U.S.P.Q. 22 (D. Ariz. 1975), *aff'd per curiam*, 591 F.2d 1278 (9th Cir. 1979) 25

Mills Music, Inc. v. Snyder, 469 U.S. 153 (1985) 97

Mirage Editions, Inc. v. Albuquerque A.R.T. Co., 856 F.2d 1341 (9th Cir. 1988) 34, 67, 68

Mitchell Brothers Film Group v. Cinema Adult Theater, 604 F.2d 852 (5th Cir. 1979) 125, 141

Mitek Holdings, Inc. v. ArcE Engineering Co., Inc, 89 F.3d 1548 (11th Cir. 1996). 23, 38

Moore v. Columbia Pictures Indus., Inc., 972 F.2d 939 (8th Cir. 1992) 106

Moorish Vanguard Concert v. Brown, 498 F. Supp. 830 (E.D. Pa. 1980) 153

Morrissey v. Procter & Gamble Co., 379 F.2d 675 (1st Cir. 1967) 10

Murray v. Gelderman, 566 F.2d 1307 (5th Cir. 1978). 42

Murray v. National Broadcasting Company, Inc., 844 F.2d 988 (2d Cir. 1988) 12

N.A.S. Import, Corp. v. Chenson Enterprises, Inc., 968 F.2d 250 (2d Cir. 1992) 148

National Basketball Assoc. Inc. v. Motorola, Inc., 105 F.3d 841 (2d Cir. 1997) 143

National Comics Publications, Inc. v. Fawcett Publications, Inc., 191 F.2d 594 (2d Cir. 1951) 140

National Football League v. McBee & Bruno's, Inc., 792 F.2d 726 (8th Cir. 1986). 3

National Rifle Assoc. of America v. Handgun Control Federation, 15 F.3d 559 (6th Cir. 1994) 131

Nelson v. Grisham, 942 F. Supp. 649 (D.D.C. 1996). 15

Nester's Map & Guide Corp. v. Hagstrom Map Co., 796 F. Supp. 729 (E.D.N.Y. 1992) 26

New Line Cinema Corp. v. Eastern Unlimited, Inc., 17 U.S.P.Q.2d 1631 (E.D.N.Y. 1989) 19

Nichols v. Universal Pictures Corp., 45 F.2d 119 (2d Cir. 1930) 14, 18

Nihon Keizai Shimbun, Inc. v. Comline Business Data, Inc., 166 F.3d 65 (2d Cir. 1999). 17, 126

Nintendo of America, Inc. v. Dragon Pacific Int'l, 40 F.3d 1007 (9th Cir. 1994) 147, 149

Oboler v. Goldin, 714 F.2d 211 (2d Cir. 1983) 146

Oddo v. Ries, 743 F.2d 630 (9th Cir. 1984) 51, 52, 104

OddzOn Products, Inc. v. Oman, 924 F.2d 346 (D.C. Cir. 1991) 29

Official Airlines Guides, Inc. v. Goss, 856 F.2d 85 (9th Cir. 1988). 151

Ohio v. Perry, 697 N.E.2d 624 (Ohio 1998) 145

On Command Video Corp. v. Columbia Pictures Indus., 777 F. Supp. 787 (N.D. Cal. 1991) 71

Original Appalachian Artworks, Inc. v. Toy Loft, Inc., 684 F.2d 821 (11th Cir. 1982) 82

P.C. Films Corp. v. MGM/UA Home Video Inc., 138 F.3d 453 (2d Cir. 1998) 55, 56

Pacific & Southern Co., Inc. v. Duncan, 744 F.2d 1490 (11th Cir. 1984) 151

Pacific and Southern Co., Inc. v. Duncan, 744 F.2d 1490 (11th Cir.1984) 119

Pamfiloff v. Giant Records, Inc., 794 F. Supp. 933 (N.D. Cal. 1992) 56

Papa's-June Music, Inc. v. McLean, 921 F. Supp. 1154 (S.D.N.Y. 1996). 53, 55

Paramount Pictures Corp. v. Doe, 821 F. Supp. 82 (E.D.N.Y. 1993) 151

Peer Int'l Corp. v. Pausa Records, Inc., 909 F.2d 1332 (9th Cir. 1990) 146, 147

Perma Greetings, Inc. v. Russ Berrie & Co., Inc., 598 F. Supp. 445 (E.D. Mo. 1984) 11

Peter Pan Fabrics, Inc. v. Martin Weiner Corp., 274 F.2d 487 (2d Cir. 1960) 107

Peter Pan Fabrics, Inc. v. Rosstex Fabrics, Inc., 733 F. Supp. 174, 177 (S.D.N.Y. 1990) 3

Philadelphia Orchestra Assoc. v. Walt Disney Co., 821 F. Supp. 341 (E.D. Pa. 1993) 42

Picture Music, Inc. v. Bourne, Inc., 457 F.2d 1213 (2d Cir.). 42

Pillsbury Co. v. Milky Way Productions, Inc., 215 U.S.P.Q. 124 (N.D. Ga. 1981) 125

Pinkham v. Camex, Inc., 84 F.3d 292 (8th Cir. 1996) 153

Plains Cotton Cooperative Ass'n v. Goodpasture Computer Service, Inc., 807 F.2d 1256 (5th Cir. 1987) 20, 150

Platinum Record Co. v. Lucasfilm, Ltd., 566 F. Supp. 226 (D.N.J. 1983) 58

Playboy Enterprises, Inc. v. Dumas, 53 F.3d 549 (2d Cir. 1995) 41, 42, 46–48

Playboy Enterprises, Inc. v. Dumas, 960 F. Supp. 710 (S.D.N.Y. 1997) 46

Playboy Enterprises, Inc. v. Frena, 839 F. Supp. 1552 (M.D. Fla. 1993) 71, 103, 125

Playboy Enterprises, Inc. v. Webbworld, Inc., 968 F. Supp. 1171 (N.D. Tex. 1997) 147

Poe v. Missing Persons, 745 F.2d 1238 (9th Cir. 1984) 26, 29

Polygram Int'l Publishing v. Nevada/TIG, Inc., 855 F. Supp. 1314 (D. Mass. 1994) 112

Powell v. Green Hill Publishers, Inc., 719 F. Supp. 743 (N.D. Ill. 1989) 138

Practice Management Information Corp. v. American Medical Ass'n, 121 F.3d 516 (9th Cir. 1997) 40, 140

PRC Realty Systems, Inc. v. National Ass'n of Realtors, 1992 Copyright L. Dec. (CCH) ¶26,961 (4th Cir. 1992) 140

Precious Moments, Inc. v. La Infantil, Inc., 971 F. Supp. 66 (D.P.R. 1997) 68

Preminger v. Columbia Pictures Corp., 267 N.Y.S.2d 594 (Sup. Ct. 1966), *aff'd*, 25 A.D.2d 830, 269 N.Y.S.2d 913 (1966), aff'd, 150 U.S.P.Q. 829 (N.Y. Ct. App. 1966) 79

Princeton University Press v. Michigan Document Services, Inc., 99 F.3d 1381 (6th Cir. 1996) 151

ProCD, Inc. v. Zeidenberg, 86 F.3d 1447 (7th Cir. 1996) 142

Prophet Music, Inc. v. Shamla Oil Co., Inc., 26 U.S.P.Q.2d 1554 (D. Minn. 1993). 72

Public Affairs Assocs. v. Rickover, 177 F. Supp. 601 (D.D.C. 1959), *rev'd on other grounds*, 284 F.2d 262 (1960), *vacated for insufficient record*, 369 U.S. 111 (1962), *on remand*, 268 F. Supp. 444 (D.D.C. 1967) 45

Publications Int'l, Ltd. v. Meredith Corp., 88 F.3d 473 (7th Cir. 1996) 10, 38

Pushman v. New York Graphic Society, Inc., 287 N.Y. 302, 39 N.E.2d 249 (1942). 41

Quality King Distributors, Inc. v. L'anza Research International, Inc., 118 S. Ct. 1125 (1998) 69

Quintanilla v. Texas Television Inc., 139 F.3d 494 (5th Cir. 1998) 43, 46, 103

Quinto v. Legal Times of Washington, Inc., 506 F. Supp. 554 (D.D.C. 1981) 35

Rano v. Sipa Press, Inc., 987 F.2d 580 (9th Cir. 1993). 93

Reader's Digest Ass'n v. Conservative Digest, Inc., 821 F.2d 800 (D.C. Cir. 1987) 5, 26, 39

Recording Industry Association of America v. Diamond Multimedia Systems Inc., 180 F.3d 1072 (9th Cir. 1999) 66

Red Baron-Granklin Park, Inc. v. Taito Corp., 883 F.2d 275 (4th Cir. 1989). 70

Religious Technology Center v. Netcom On-Line Communication Services, Inc., 907 F. Supp. 1361 (N.D. Cal. 1995). 104, 111, 112

Repp v. Webber, 132 F.3d 882 (2d Cir. 1997) 107

Respect Inc. v. Committee on the Status of Women, 821 F. Supp. 531 (N.D. Ill. 1993). 46

Rexnord, Inc. v. Modern Handling Systems, Inc., 379 F. Supp. 1190 (D. Del. 1974) 14

Rey v. Lafferty, 990 F.2d 1379 (1st Cir. 1993). 57, 59

Reyher v. Children's Television Workshop, 533 F.2d 87 (2d Cir.) 18

Richard Feiner and Co. v. Turner Ent. Co., 98 F.3d 33 (2d Cir. 1996) 150, 151

Richmond v. Weiner, 353 F.2d 41 (9th Cir. 1965) 52
Ringgold v. Black Entertainment Television, 126 F.3d 70 (2d Cir. 1997) 109, 119, 135
Robert R. Jones Assoc., Inc. v. Nino Homes, 858 F.2d 274 (6th Cir.1988) 146
Rodrigue v. Rodrigue, 50 U.S.P.Q.2d 1278 (E.D. La. 1999) 52
Rodriguez v. Texas Commission on the Arts, 992 F. Supp. 876 (N.D. Tex. 1998) 104
Rogers v. Koons, 960 F.2d 301, 310 (2d Cir.) 126
Roley v. New World Pictures, Ltd., 19 F.3d 479 (9th Cir. 1994) 139
Rooney v. Columbia Pictures Industries, Inc., 538 F. Supp. 211 (S.D.N.Y.), *aff'd*, 714 F.2d 117 (2d Cir. 1982) 58
Rosemont Enterprises, Inc. v. Random House, Inc., 366 F.2d 303 (2d Cir. 1966) 17, 128, 131, 132
Rosette v. Rainbo Record Mfg. Corp., 354 F. Supp. 1183 (S.D.N.Y. 1973), *aff'd per curiam*, 546 F.2d 461 (2d Cir. 1976) 80
Roth v. Pritikin, 710 F.2d 934, 938-39 (2d Cir. 1983) 42
S.O.S., Inc. v. Payday, Inc., 886 F.2d 1081 (9th Cir. 1989) 50, 137
Saenger Organization, Inc. v. Nationwide Ins. Licensing Assoc., Inc., 119 F.3d 55 (1st Cir. 1997) 43
Sailor Music v. Gap Stores, Inc., 668 F.2d 84 (7th Cir. 1981) 71
Salinger v. Random House, Inc., 811 F.2d 90 (2d Cir. 1987) 13, 40
Salinger v. Random House, Inc., 818 F.2d 252 (2d Cir. 1987) 17, 126–128, 131
Sampson & Murdock Co. v. Seaver-Radford Co., 140 F. 539 (1st Cir. 1905) 129
Sandoval v. New Line Cinema Corp., 147 F.3d 215 (2d Cir. 1998) 109, 135
Sandoval v. New Line Cinema Corp., 973 F. Supp. 409, *aff'd*, 147 F.3d 215 (2d Cir. 1998) 135

Santrayll v. Burrell, 39 U.S.P.Q.2d 1052 (S.D.N.Y. 1996) 8

Saxon v. Blann, 968 F.2d 676 (8th Cir. 1992) 55

SBK Catalogue Partnership v. Orion Pictures Corp., 723 F. Supp. 1053 (D.N.J. 1989) 138

Scherr v. Universal Match Corp., 417 F.2d 497 (2d Cir. 1969) 5, 39, 44

Schiller & Schmidt, Inc. v. Nordisco Corp., 969 F.2d 410 (7th Cir. 1992) 47, 55

Schnapper v. Foley, 667 F. 2d 102 (D.C. Cir. 1981). 40

Schoenberg v. Shapolsky Publishers, Inc., 971 F.2d 926 (2d Cir. 1992) 102

Sega Enterprises Ltd. v. Accolade, Inc., 977 F.2d 1510 (9th Cir. 1993) 21, 23

Selle v. Gibb, 741 F.2d 896 (7th Cir. 1984) 106

Selznick v. Turner Entertainment Co., 990 F. Supp. 1180 (C.D. Cal. 1997) 102

Seminole Tribe of Florida v. Florida, 517 U.S. 44 (1995) 104

Shapiro, Bernstein & Co., Inc. v. H.L. Green Co., Inc., 316 F.2d 304 (2d Cir. 1963) 112

Shaw v. Lindheim, 809 F. Supp. 1393 (C.D. Cal. 1992) 106

Shaw v. Lindheim, 908 F.2d 531 (9th Cir. 1990). 14, 19, 108

Shaw v. Lindheim, 919 F.2d 1353 (9th Cir. 1990). 11

Sheldon v. Metro-Goldwyn Pictures Corp., 81 F.2d 49 (2d Cir. 1936) 5, 14, 108, 110

Shipman v. RKO Pictures, 100 F.2d 533 (2d Cir. 1938) 14

Sid & Marty Krofft Television Productions, Inc. v. McDonald's Corp., 562 F.2d 1157 (9th Cir. 1977). 108

Siegel v. National Periodical Pubs., Inc., 508 F.2d 909 (2d Cir. 1974) 55

Silverman v. CBS, Inc., 870 F.2d 40 (2d Cir. 1989) 18

Sony Computer Entertainment Inc. v. Connectix Corp., 48 F. Supp. 2d 1212 (N.D. Cal. 1999). 23

Sony Corp. of America v. Universal City Studios, Inc., 464 U.S. 417 (1984) 1, 117, 120–122, 128, 130, 136

Sony Music Entertainment, Inc., v. Global Arts Productions, 45 F. Supp. 2d 1345 (S.D. Fla. 1999) 150

Soptra Fabrics Corp. v. Stafford Knitting Mills, Inc., 490 F.2d 1092 (2d Cir. 1974) 27

Southern Bell Tel. & Tel. v. Associated Tel. Directory Publishers, 756 F.2d 801 (11th Cir. 1985) 104

Springsteen v. Plaza Roller Dome, Inc., 602 F. Supp. 1113 (M.D.N.C. 1985) 72

Steinberg v. Columbia Pictures Industries, Inc., 663 F. Supp. 706 (S.D.N.Y. 1987) 109

Stern Electronics, Inc. v. Kaufman, 669 F.2d 852 (2d Cir. 1982) 22, 30

Stevens Linen Associates, Inc. v. Mastercraft Corp., 656 F.2d 11 (2d Cir. 1981) 145

Stewart v. Abend, 495 U.S. 207 (1990) 89, 122, 125

Stone v. Williams, 970 F.2d 1043 (2d Cir. 1992) 139

Streeter v. Rolfe, 491 F. Supp. 416 (W.D. La. 1980) 11

Subafilms, Ltd. v. MGM-Pathe Communications Co., 24 F.3d 1088 (9th Cir. 1994) 63, 103, 111

Sundeman v. The Seajay Society, Inc., 142 F.3d 194 (4th Cir. 1998) 126, 127, 130, 132

Superior Form Builders v. Dan Chase Taxidermy, 74 F.3d 488 (4th Cir. 1996) 28

Sylvestre v. Oswald, Copyright L. Dec. (CCH) ¶27,120 (S.D.N.Y. 1993) 107

Synercom Technology, Inc. v. University Computing Co., 462 F. Supp. 1003 (N.D. Tex. 1978) 20

Synercom Technology, Inc. v. University Computing Co., 474 F. Supp. 37 (N.D. Tex. 1979) 141

Synergistic Technologies, Inc. v. IDB Mobile Communications, Inc., 871 F. Supp. 24 (D.D.C. 1994) 25

Systems XIX, Inc. v. Parker, 30 F. Supp. 2d 1225 (N.D. Cal. 1998) 49, 50, 54, 144

T.B. Harms Co. v. Eliscu, 339 F.2d 823 (2d Cir. 1964) 102

Tasini v. New York Times Co., 1999 WL 753966 (2d Cir. Sept. 24, 1999) 35, 64, 68, 70

Taylor v. Meirick, 712 F.2d 1112 (7th Cir. 1983) 139

Ted Arnold Ltd. v. Silvercraft Co., 259 F. Supp. 733 (S.D.N.Y. 1966) 29

Tele-Pac, Inc. v. Grainger, 570 N.Y.S.2d 521, *appeal dismissed*, 580 N.Y.S.2d 201, 588 N.E.2d 99 (1991) 58

Tempo Music, inc. v. Famous Music Corp., 838 F. Supp. 162 (S.D.N.Y. 1994) 8, 9

Thomson v. Larson, 147 F.3d 195 (2d Cir. 1998) 49, 50

Time, Inc. v. Bernard Geis Associates, 293 F. Supp. 130 (S.D.N.Y. 1968) 7, 131

Tom Doherty Assocs., Inc. v. Saban Entertainment, Inc., 60 F.3d 27 (2d Cir. 1995) 151

Toro Co. v. R & R Products Co., 787 F.2d 1208 (8th Cir. 1986) 37

Towler v. Sayles, 76 F.3d 579 (4th Cir. 1996) 106

Trandes Corp. v. Guy F. Atkinson Co., 996 F.2d 655 (4th Cir. 1993) 142

Trenton v. Infinity Broadcasting Corp., 865 F. Supp. 1416 (C.D. Cal. 1994) 11

Triangle Publications, Inc. v. Knight-Ridder Newspapers, Inc., 626 F.2d 1171 (5th Cir. 1980) 110, 138

Twentieth Century Music Corp. v. Aiken, 422 U.S. 151 (1975) 72

Twin Books Corp. v. Walt Disney Co., 83 F.3d 1162 (9th Cir. 1996) 4, 81

Twin Peaks Productions, Inc. v. Publications Int'l, Inc., 996 F.2d 1366 (2d Cir. 1993) 120, 148

United Feature Syndicate, Inc. v. Sunrise Mold Co., Inc., 569 F. Supp. 1475 (S.D. Fla. 1983) 149

United States ex rel. Berge v. Board of Trustees of Univ. of Alabama, 104 F.3d 1453 (4th Cir. 1997) 142, 144

United States v. Hamilton, 583 F.2d 448 (9th Cir. 1978). 26

United States v. Moghadam, 175 F.3d 1269 (11th Cir. 1999). 4

United States v. Shabazz, 724 F.2d 1536 11th Cir. 1984) 139

Universal City Studios, Inc. v. Kamar Industries, Inc., 217 U.S.P.Q. 1162 (S.D. Tex. 1982) 12

Update Art, Inc. v. Modiin Publ'g, Ltd., 843 F.2d 67 (2d Cir. 1988) 63, 146

Urantia Foundation v. Maaherra, 895 F. Supp. 1329 (D. Ariz. 1995) 138

Urantia Foundation v. Maaherra, 114 F.3d 955 (9th Cir. 1997). 5

Valente-Kritzer Video v. Pinckney, 881 F.2d 772 (9th Cir. 1989) 142

Value Group, Inc. v. Mendham Lake Estates, L.P., 800 F. Supp. 1228 (D.N.J. 1992). 150

Vault Corp. v. Quaid Software, 847 F.2d 255 (5th Cir. 1988). 142

Venus Music Corp. v. Mills Music, Inc., 261 F.2d 577 (2d Cir. 1958) 56

Vestron, Inc v. Home Box Office Inc., 839 F.2d 1380 (9th Cir. 1988) 102

Victor Lalli Enters., Inc. v. Big Red Apple, Inc., 936 F.2d 671 (2d Cir. 1991) 37

Wainwright Securities Inc. v. Wall Street Transcript Corp., 558 F.2d 91 (2d Cir. 1977) 17

Waits v. Frito-Lay, Inc., 978 F.2d 1093 (9th Cir. 1992). 142

Walt Disney Co. v. Powell, 897 F.2d 565 (D.C. Cir.1990) 149

Walt Disney Productions v. Air Pirates, 581 F.2d 751 (9th Cir. 1978). 18, 128, 131, 135, 138

Walt Disney Productions v. Filmation Associates, 628 F. Supp. 871 (C.D. Cal. 1986) 63

Walt Disney Productions v. Mature Pictures Corp., 389 F. Supp. 1397 (S.D.N.Y. 1975) 124

Walthal v. Rusk, 172 F.3d 481 (7th Cir. 1999) 93

Warner Bros. Pictures, Inc. v. Columbia Broadcasting System, Inc., 216 F.2d 945 (9th Cir. 1954) 19

Warner Bros., Inc. v. American Broadcasting Companies, Inc., 523 F. Supp. 611 (S.D.N.Y.), *aff'd*, 654 F.2d 204 (2d Cir. 1981) 123

Warner Brothers. v. American Broadcasting Companies, 654 F.2d 204 (2d Cir. 1981). 108

Warner Bros., Inc. v. American Broadcasting Companies., 720 F.2d 231 (2d Cir. 1983) 18

Warren Publishing, Inc. v. Microdos Data Corp., 115 F.3d 1509 (11th Cir.1997) 36, 149

Weissmann v. Freeman, 868 F.2d 1313 (2d Cir. 1989) 49

Weitzenkorn v. Lesser, 40 Cal. 2d 778, 256 P.2d 947 (1953) 13

Werbungs und Commerz Union Austalt v. LeShufy, 6 U.S.P.Q.2d 1153 (S.D.N.Y. 1987) 51

West Publ'g Co. v. Mead Data Central, Inc., 799 F.2d 1219 (8th Cir. 1986) 38

Weygand v. CBS, Inc., Copyright L. Rep. (CCH) ¶27,660 (C.D. Cal. 1997) 106

WGN Continental Broadcasting Co. v. United Video, Inc., 693 F.2d 622 (7th Cir. 1982). 29

Wheaton v. Peters, 33 U.S. (8 Pet.) 591 (1834) 40

Whelan Associates, Inc. v. Jaslow Dental Laboratory, Inc., 797 F.2d 1222 (3d Cir. 1986) 20

Whimsicality, Inc. v. Rubie's Costume Co., 891 F.2d 452 (2d Cir. 1989) 29

White v. Kimmell, 193 F.2d 744 (9th Cir. 1952) 81

Wihtol v. Crow, 309 F.2d 777 (9th Cir. 1962) 128

Williams v. Crichton, 84 F.3d 589 (2d Cir. 1996) 15, 109

Wojnarowicz v. American Family Association, 745 F. Supp. 130 (S.D.N.Y. 1990) 79

Woods v. Bourne Co., 60 F.3d 978 (2d Cir. 1995) 97

Words & Data, Inc. v. GTE Communications, Inc., 765 F. Supp. 570 (W.D. Mo. 1991) 50

Worlds of Wonder, Inc. v. Veritel Learning Systems, Inc., 658 F. Supp. 351 (N.D. Tex. 1986) 30

Wright v. Warner Books, Inc., 953 F.2d 731 (2d Cir. 1991) 123

Yount v. Acuff Rose-Opryland, 103 F.3d 830 (9th Cir. 1996) 103

Zuill v. Shanahan, 80 F.3d 1366 (9th Cir. 1996) 139

Appendix B

Table of Statutes

U.S. Const. art. I, § 8 1
17 U.S.C. § 102 141
17 U.S.C. § 102(a) 2, 4
17 U.S.C. § 102(a)(4) 25
17 U.S.C. § 102(a)(5) 33
17 U.S.C. § 102(a)(8) 31, 33
17 U.S.C. § 102(b) 9, 10
17 U.S.C. § 103 . . . . 34, 35, 141
17 U.S.C. § 103(a) 35
17 U.S.C. § 103(b) 35
17 U.S.C. § 104 59
17 U.S.C. § 104A 60, 69
17 U.S.C. § 104A(d)(1). 62
17 U.S.C. §§ 104A(d)(2). 62
17 U.S.C. § 105 . . . . 39, 40
17 U.S.C. § 106 . . . . 63, 145
17 U.S.C. § 106(1) 63
17 U.S.C. § 106(2) 67
17 U.S.C. § 106(3) 68
17 U.S.C. § 106(4) 70
17 U.S.C. § 106(5) 75
17 U.S.C. § 106(6) 75
17 U.S.C. § 106A 76
17 U.S.C. § 106A(a) 77
17 U.S.C. § 106A(a)(3)(A) 77
17 U.S.C. § 106A(a)(3)(B) 77
17 U.S.C. § 106A(c) 77

17 U.S.C. § 106A(d)(1) 79
17 U.S.C. § 106A(d)(2) 79
17 U.S.C. § 106A(e) 79
17 U.S.C. § 107 . . . . . 119, 126
17 U.S.C. § 108 64
17 U.S.C. § 109(a) 68, 69
17 U.S.C. § 109(b)(1) 69
17 U.S.C. § 109(c) 75
17 U.S.C. § 110(1) 74
17 U.S.C. § 110(4) 74
17 U.S.C. § 110(5) 72
17 U.S.C. § 110(5)(B) 72
17 U.S.C. § 110(7) 74
17 U.S.C. § 112 64
17 U.S.C. § 112(a)(2) 65
17 U.S.C. § 113(a) 27
17 U.S.C. § 113(c) 29
17 U.S.C. § 113(d) 78
17 U.S.C. § 113(d)(1)(B) 78
17 U.S.C. § 113(d)(2) 78
17 U.S.C. § 113(d)(2)(A) 78
17 U.S.C. § 113(d)(2)(B) 78
17 U.S.C. § 114 74
17 U.S.C. § 114(d)(1) 75
17 U.S.C. § 114(d)(2) 75
17 U.S.C. § 114(d)(3) 75
17 U.S.C. § 114(g)(2) 76
17 U.S.C. § 114(h) 75
17 U.S.C. § 115 . . . . . 25, 65
17 U.S.C. § 115(c)(3)(A) 65
17 U.S.C. § 115(c)(3)(E) 65
17 U.S.C. § 117 . . . . . 23–25, 65
17 U.S.C. § 117(c) 24, 64
17 U.S.C. § 120(a) 32
17 U.S.C. § 120(b) 33

17 U.S.C. § 201(a) 41, 51
17 U.S.C. § 201(b) 5, 41, 44, 46
17 U.S.C. § 201(c) 35, 36, 64, 68, 70, 85
17 U.S.C. § 201(d) 52
17 U.S.C. § 202 40
17 U.S.C. § 203 90
17 U.S.C. § 203(a)(2) 92
17 U.S.C. § 203(a)(3) 93
17 U.S.C. § 203(a)(5) 95
17 U.S.C. § 203(b)(1) 91
17 U.S.C. § 203(b)(3) 94
17 U.S.C. § 203(b)(4) 95
17 U.S.C. § 203(b)(6) 95
17 U.S.C. § 204 53
17 U.S.C. § 205 56
17 U.S.C. § 205(d) 56
17 U.S.C. § 301 141
17 U.S.C. § 301(b)(4) 33
17 U.S.C. § 301(c) 31, 145
17 U.S.C. § 301(f) 80
17 U.S.C. § 302(a) 86
17 U.S.C. § 302(b) 87
17 U.S.C. § 302(c) 87
17 U.S.C. § 303 87
17 U.S.C. § 303(b) 81
17 U.S.C. § 304 88
17 U.S.C. § 304(a) 88, 101
17 U.S.C. § 304(a)(1)(C) 88
17 U.S.C. § 304(b) 90
17 U.S.C. § 304(c) 95, 96
17 U.S.C. § 304(c)(2) 97
17 U.S.C. § 304(c)(5) 100
17 U.S.C. § 304(c)(6)(A) 97
17 U.S.C. § 304(c)(6)(D) 100
17 U.S.C. § 304(d) 98, 100, 101

17 U.S.C. § 401(a) 82
17 U.S.C. § 401(d) 84, 147
17 U.S.C. § 402(d) 84, 147
17 U.S.C. § 404(a) 85
17 U.S.C. § 405 82
17 U.S.C. § 405(b) 83
17 U.S.C. § 406(a) 83
17 U.S.C. § 407 . . . . 85, 86
17 U.S.C. § 410(c) 86, 105
17 U.S.C. § 411 85
17 U.S.C. § 411(a) 103
17 U.S.C. § 412 . . . . 62, 147, 152
17 U.S.C. § 501(b) 101
17 U.S.C. § 502 149
17 U.S.C. § 503 151
17 U.S.C. § 504 104
17 U.S.C. § 504(c) 146
17 U.S.C. § 504(c)(1) 149
17 U.S.C. § 504(c)(2) 147
17 U.S.C. § 504(d) 74
17 U.S.C. § 505 152
17 U.S.C. § 506(a) 117
17 U.S.C. § 507 139
17 U.S.C. § 507(a) 117
17 U.S.C. § 511 104
17 U.S.C. § 512 . . . . 74, 113
17 U.S.C. § 512(a) 113
17 U.S.C. § 512(b) 114
17 U.S.C. § 512(c) 114
17 U.S.C. § 512(c)(2) 114
17 U.S.C. § 512(c)(3) 115
17 U.S.C. § 512(d) 115
17 U.S.C. § 512(d)(3) 115
17 U.S.C. § 512(g) 116
17 U.S.C. § 512(h) 117

17 U.S.C. § 512(i) 113
17 U.S.C. § 512(j) 114–116
17 U.S.C. § 512(k) 113
17 U.S.C. § 901 22
17 U.S.C. § 1004 66
17 U.S.C. § 1006 .... 66, 67
17 U.S.C. § 1008 .... 66, 136
17 U.S.C. § 1101 .... 4, 64, 70, 74
17 U.S.C. § 1201 .... 153, 156, 157
17 U.S.C. § 1201(a) 153
17 U.S.C. § 1201(b) 153
17 U.S.C. § 1201(c) 154
17 U.S.C. § 1201(d) 154
17 U.S.C. § 1201(e) 154
17 U.S.C. § 1201(f) 23, 154
17 U.S.C. § 1201(g) 154
17 U.S.C. § 1201(h) 154
17 U.S.C. § 1201(i) 155
17 U.S.C. § 1201(j) 155
17 U.S.C. § 1201(k) 155
17 U.S.C. § 1202 .... 155, 156, 157
17 U.S.C. § 1202(a) 155
17 U.S.C. § 1202(b) 155
17 U.S.C. § 1202(c) 155
17 U.S.C. § 1202(d) 156
17 U.S.C. § 1202(e) 156
17 U.S.C. § 1203 156
17 U.S.C. § 1204 157
18 U.S.C. § 2319 117
18 U.S.C. § 2319A 4
28 U.S.C. § 1338(a) 102
28 U.S.C. § 4001 53
Cal. Civ. Code § 980(a)(1) 2
Cal. Civ. Code § 987 79
Cal. Civ. Code § 989 79

Mass. Gen Laws Ann. ch. 231, § 855 79
N.Y. Arts & Cultural Affairs Law § 14.51 79